A Hybrid in America

A Hybrid in America

Leoda Buckwalter

Evangel Publishing House
Nappanee, Indiana 46550

Cover Design: Tracey Owen

Library of Congress Catalog Card No. 98-72639

ISBN: 0-916035-86-7

Printed in the United States of America

3 2 1

To you, Christine Lawson,
fellow hybrid and free spirit,
my dear beloved sister in Jesus Christ,
because you, too,
choose to bloom wherever
the Master Gardener plants you.

Contents

INTRODUCTION

Writing this assessment of the past sixteen years in the light of more than fifty years lived abroad has been another great learning experience for me. My first lesson surprised me: I am no authority on America! I am yet a learner. American life and thought patterns are still planting their fertile impressions deep into my spirit. So this book is fresh, and I trust, invigorating.

I have a story to tell, one that has grown out of my past and leads into my future. It is up-to-date, very relevant to today's changing scene. But, with a ratio of fifty years lived abroad to sixteen adult years in the United States since retirement, when looking for illustrations, my past rushed forward. Spiritual lessons learned in India form the basis for what God, my heavenly Father, is teaching me now. If you have already read my last book, *Confessions of a Hybrid—My Spiritual Journey* (published by Evangel Publishing House, 1996), you will find this a natural sequel.

But, welcome to all newcomers, too! For you, a word of explanation about those fifty years will help. I call myself a "hybrid" because two strong strains comprise who I am today. My first eleven years of childhood not only began in India, but formed the broad base for my future ministry in that same subcontinent, a period covering almost forty-two years. It was shared by my husband, Allen Buckwalter, who first saw India on November 20, 1939. We officially retired on May 1, 1981.

In between came seven terms of service of varying length, the first twenty years spent in village India, and the latter twenty-two years with a new ministry arm—missionary radio. During the years when boat travel was cheap, we spent up to seven weeks en route to our homeland. When plane travel came into vogue, the new time schedule shattered the old one!

9

A lifetime of adaptations, therefore, undergirds Allen and me now in these final days of change. That, I believe, is a blessing. So is the fact that a third dominating strand in my story binds it together to make me capable of writing at the age of eighty-two. As an octogenarian, then, now living in the United States, I come to you with some of the discoveries that I am now in the process of learning:

1. America is full of "hybrids"—people who represent two or more cultures. Most of us seem to have come from somewhere else, either by moving from one part of the country to another, or because our forefathers immigrated from abroad to this great land. In opening her doors to the homeless, the downtrodden, the refugees, and those seeking security, the United States welcomes, nurtures, and helps to make their dreams come true. This is a great land!

2. All of us are a product of our past. In an intricate society, based on the worth of the individual, potential beauty and richness run parallel with multitudinous problems that also arise. This democratic form of government rests, how securely may be a matter of conjecture, on foundational truth in the Holy Bible. Our founding fathers and we have a Judeo-Christian heritage. As a result, God has richly blessed us as a nation.

3. To merge in, then, is the challenge. All of us here have something unique to offer, over and above our right to vote. But we must first be willing to open ourselves to others— believing in our own worth and the inestimable worth of those around us. Whether or not we do this depends on choice, our own choice!

4. The right of choice is ours, a right given to us by God, our Creator. The path we choose will likely be determined by circumstance, but many stories of the human spirit overcoming all types of hindrances thrill not only the American public, but the world!

5. God, our Creator, has given us the right of choice, true, but God alone reserves the authority to determine the results of those choices. Being a God of love, as well as holy and righteous in all his ways, God gives us warnings and directives in his Word, the Holy Bible. These are non-negotiables. We may break ourselves on the laws of God, but we can never change God's laws!

6. In this land of opportunity, we usually take one of three paths: doing our "own thing," following some leader whose charisma ensnares us, or following the truth as found in the Word of God. In other words, we are like "sheep without a shepherd." That was Jesus Christ's estimation of the people around him when he walked the shores of Galilee. What would he say now?

To me, following the genuine rather than the counterfeit is crucial, and I write from this perspective. Being a teacher rather than an evangelist, I find illustrative material very easy to remember. So you will read numerous stories taken either from personal experience or the witness of other "hybrids" like me.

Grateful thanks to all who have encouraged me in this task. Many of my peers answered my queries concerning their feelings and reactions in cross-cultural living. Not only did they answer, but went into detail, showing me that my individual problems on re-entry were not unusual. I trust this book is helpful to every one who has been able to identify.

Personal thanks, also, to Christine Lawson, to Virginia Weaver, and to Harriet Bert who read and critiqued either part of the manuscript or the whole. Each has encouraged me tremendously. Chris, in being an African-American and a dear sister in the Lord, opened my eyes to the vast numbers who can identify with the feelings I had upon reentry.

My husband Allen, with whom I have shared sixty-one years of marriage, is a bulwark for sound advice and constant support. My daughter and family also have made this work of faith and labor of love possible. And lastly, I must mention those stalwarts, the members of our warm-hearted church fellowship in Elizabethtown, Pa., who have prayed earnestly for us, proving their Christian love by countless acts of kindness. Why? Because in Jesus Christ there is neither east nor west, male nor female, high nor low—but Christ is *all* and *in all*. To him be the final thanks and praise.

Leoda Buckwalter
Mechanicsburg, Pennsylvania

CHAPTER ONE

A MATTER OF IDENTITY

Some twenty years ago my husband and I stood hungrily before our first-ever vending machine in Kennedy Airport. Wondering how to procure a tempting cup of steaming hot coffee and a delicious sandwich displayed behind glass, we tried to assimilate the directions, but frankly, we were having some trouble.

I finally turned to an amused bystander and said, "Sir, would you help us please? We've never seen a machine like this before."

"Oh?" He seemed startled. Perhaps he thought us touched with senility since we were elderly, or perhaps we had come from another country. I felt embarrassed. However, he did help us, and we learned another lesson in adjusting culturally to a new environment. It was the first of many more to come.

Where had we been? Ten thousand miles away, living in New Delhi, India, the capital city of a great nation situated on the other side of the world. Moreover, India boasts a five-thousand-year-old culture!

In Delhi we were engaged in missionary radio, producing programs for shortwave broadcasting over Christian radio stations owned and operated (outside India) by Far East Broadcasting International. Our network of recording studios sent sixty programs every week to our FEBA India headquarters. Allen's administrative responsibility and my follow-up and public relations appointment kept us more than busy.

Prior to living and working in the great cities of Bangalore and then Delhi, we had already spent twenty years in missionary work in rural North Bihar, where I was born of American parentage. India was my home!

No vending machines there? Not then; maybe now, but my guess is that they're found in very limited quantities. I know vendors still call their wares, plying their trade in cities and villages alike, certainly on railroad station platforms. We learned early to appreciate the hot, spicy food sold for a pittance, and to buy discriminately. But buy we did!

During the latter part of our forty years in India, we found new technological advances facing us every time we returned to the States for home leave. Hotels and airports en route made us aware of new features: TV sets, paper towels displacing linens, knobs and buttons to push. One day in a Japanese airport, when I desired to dry my hands, I found neither a handle nor a button! Now what should I do? By chance I placed my hands under the dryer and automatically a rush of hot air hit them. This particular convenience soon found its way to America as well.

While Allen finished business in Calcutta at the end of our final term in India, I spent a week at "Edgehill," a missionary guest house in Landour, Mussoorie, near Woodstock School in the lower Himalayas. Managed by our English friends, Colonel and Mrs. Norrish, it provided a wonderful vacation home for a multi-national group. Being there, I saw an unforgettable program given in the Community Centre. The name of the play was aptly termed "Innocence Returns." The appreciative audience of perhaps two hundred missionaries, representing almost every nation of the western world, laughed hilariously as memories came alive. Why? We were laughing at ourselves!

One scene showed a harried mother of five children arriving by ship on home leave. She led her family down the gangplank and across the wharf with her babe in arms, the omnipresent shoulder bag slung over her shoulder. Behind her came her brood of "Indian Americans," walking single file, as they had always seen Indians do. Each child carried his or her suitcase balanced on their heads! No wonder the Americans were amused.

A seasoned missionary was shown in the busy Union Central Station, standing helplessly and calling, "Coolie! Coolie!" (Had Aunt Effie actually done that? She said she had.) I laughed with abandon as I recalled our Kennedy Airport incident, and about the time I took my first plane ride in America.

Despite some trepidation, I had enjoyed the flight from Los Angeles to Washington, D.C., and hoped my host family from Waynesboro, Pa., could meet me. They didn't! I had to find a bus. But which one? How would I know? I asked a porter, who looked at me as though something was wrong with me. "Ma'am," he said hurrying by, "the shuttle bus is waiting outside to take you to the main terminal in town." I felt hot. I should have known, but I didn't. If I had not looked like an American he would have guessed I was a stranger.

In our orientation to modern America, we have now learned that such mistakes are called "bloopers." During that week at "Edgehill" when we laughed at our own foibles, we didn't even know the word. But one thing was sure. We could expect trouble when we tried to reenter the western world after having lived forty years abroad, and we were right. I remember a day's bus trip from Buffalo, N.Y., to Harrisburg, Pa. Alone, since Allen had stayed in India while I came to the States for two months in 1979, I was afraid to get off the bus to eat because I would have to work a vending machine.

Thought patterns in cross-cultural transitions must change! We left India in 1981 to retire, but we learned that thought and behavior routines don't change overnight. It takes a conscious effort, like keeping a New Year's resolution. In reentry, as when anyone first arrives in a foreign culture, we had to push our way through four different stages of adjustment. Let me share these four with you.

The first is *curiosity*. A visitor "loves" the novelty of something different, eye-catching. In Delhi, where we lived for thirteen years, we often saw tourists snapping pictures profusely of the slum areas, bypassing all the well-built condominiums nearby. Even when we tried to tell them, they failed to note that such slum dwellers were usually transported villagers who were working for a daily wage on this new building site.

We also noted that newcomers were fascinated by private life lived in public. "It's so quaint," they would say, and return home with pictures of station platforms, bathing ghats with masses of pilgrims, anything different from what they had known at home. Come to think of it, we did the same—at least my husband did. He's the photographer in our family. But, whereas his pictures focused on the "curious" in those early years, now they feature beautiful Indian faces and magnificent scenery. Interesting!

Tourists come, and tourists go, taking their impressions and pictures with them. When the foreigner stays for a year or two the curiosity often gives way to the second stage, *comparison*. He or she begins to compare this new life with the one left behind. Depending on the outlook, this can become an exercise in futility that tends to serious homesickness or sometimes downright despair, as is often the case in first-term missionaries.

But there are stalwarts who push bravely through. Some find the new life a challenge that leads to stage three, *conflict*. If the foreigner can progress to this third stage without returning home, it is still uncertain as to whether he or she will fit into the host culture. Why?

At odds with the new surroundings, now the newcomer may try to change people and customs, and may (or may not) succeed. British colonizers stayed in India long enough to establish a remarkable civil service arm of administration. It greatly aided in stabilizing a seething subcontinent through years of political fluidity following India's independence from Britain in 1947. The colonists also bequeathed to the new nation a marvelous train system that crisscrosses the otherwise ethnically divided country. Those trains have done much to unify the Republic.

Changes coming from conflict can be either beneficial or detrimental, as illustrated in North Bihar where we lived for twenty years. Large areas of farmland were being reclaimed from devastation caused by the raging Kosi River. Well-meaning western philanthropists donated tractors to replace the time-honored hand-driven plow. Plowing deeper than the older plows, the tractors turned up sand, burying the rich surface loam left by silting. Once again the land became useless. Rusted tractors told this sad tale of change gone awry.

So conflict can lead to failure, especially when the West tries to conform the East to its patterns of modernity. However, beneficial changes do come at times, as in the case of India producing its own aircraft, precision watches, and finding useful new methods of farming under the tutelage of foreign countries.

A hilarious story of conflict comes from an Indian newspaper we regularly receive. We knew that in the 1990s, the TV craze had gripped India. But something had recently happened in a suburb of Bombay which caused Allen and me to pause and wonder. In July of 1995 we opened the *Forerunner* to read an article captioned: "Throwing Out the Idiot Box." We learned that hundreds of Indians, sick of violence and sex on television, had actually hurled their TV sets out of the windows of two high-rise buildings in the fashionable Bombay neighborhood of Versova. Why? Because one night a Muslim lady, Safira Ali Mohammad, and her family carried their television set to the window and threw it out! She told the reporter, "There was a tremendous crash. Many neighbors also pushed their television set out of the window. We set the trend."

This destruction of television sets in two large apartment buildings in Bombay came as a result of rising criticism that Indian and Western soap operas, game shows, and dance sequences were increasingly violent and indecent, an offense to Indian viewers and their families. They certainly found a way of solving their problem! When East duels with the West, there's conflict for sure. In my estimation, in this case the Muslim ladies who desire to hold family values high won the contest.

Yes, we laughed. But when I asked my husband whether he was going to throw our television set out the window, he didn't take kindly to the suggestion. Rather, he uses the off-button to screen out that which is vulgar and not worth watching. He's an American. We solve things differently here than do people on the other side of the world.

Conflict over these cultural differences may continue over a long period of time, with much fluidity. We have Anglo-Indian friends living in village India who still wear western garb though their surroundings push them into an Indian mold. They, too, are a "neither-nor" species, as am I.

Placed in an American setting, this continuation of "foreign behavior patterns" reminds me of a mission organization's centennial celebration here in the States. Originally from Germany, their planning utilized a brass band in the Sunday morning worship service! Very German! And the picnic afterwards featured all German foods, except for the dessert which was delicious American icecream. Apparently they still hold close ties with the homeland.

Adaptability has become a way of life here. Many immigrants do as we try to do—simply turn a page when leaving their past. Those who do this quickly become Americans. Eventually the game of pitting Eastern and Western behavior patterns diminishes. In the fourth stage, the person involved either *complies*, lays down arms and becomes part of the host culture, or with a weary sigh of relief, *withdraws* and returns home. And "home" looks good, oh, so good! At least for awhile such persons are content, until the reasons which took them away in the first place become so strong that second and third thoughts eventually show the returnees that this, too, has lost its charm. What happens then? We have misfits, people who are unhappy in either place, because the years and experiences have made every one of us what we are. We become a product of our past.

Place the above struggle for adaptability to a host culture into a broader setting where one is dealing not with individuals but with communities, and the results differ. Rarely will communities get up and leave. Instead, they tend to cling to their differences, making them unique in their setting. The Amish in Pennsylvania, Ohio, and Indiana provide classic examples. Los Angeles and Miami exude Spanish influence, and Brooklyn in New York City has its Jewish culture. I could give other examples, but resist the temptation to do so.

Expatriates abroad often cling to those distinctives that make them unique. Britishers like their "tea," the Anglican liturgy, or the Keswick Hymnal. Scots enjoy singing psalms and Irish love their ballads. What about the Americans? Do we have our distinctives, too? Yes, I am sure we do. How about food, shopping sprees, and fast service?

One time in Kalimpong, a delightful mountain resort in the lower Himalayas, Allen and I attended a picnic. We were the only

Allen and Leoda with Indian friends in Chicago.

Americans among these missionaries from all parts of the United
Kingdom. Whereas others worried about taking a teakettle, crum-
pets, and scones, we looked for a field of luxurious sweet corn.
Finding it, Allen bought fresh corn on the cob to roast for the picnic. It made a big hit! The American in us was showing.

Walking down the main street on our only visit to Kuala Lumpur
in Malaysia, we suddenly stopped. In front of us was a picture of
Colonel Sanders, and a sign announced that you could buy Ken-
tucky Fried Chicken inside the restaurant. Could we resist that
temptation? Never! We ate heartily and relished every bite, because
it represented "home" to us. At that juncture, Allen and I were very
American.

Another time, it was McDonalds in Hong Kong that stopped our
busy schedule. And so it goes. Right now, as I work on this chapter, I am wearing a Kashmiri *kameez* (tunic) that seems just right for
a cold day in Pennsylvania. Our spice rack carries two kinds of
curry powder and is well filled with other spices. And in a cupboard
is my prize—a bag of *mokhana*, a finger food that undoubtedly
comes from India, and probably from my home state of Bihar! You
see, in America there is still a great deal of the "Indian" in me.

Adaptability may bring an interesting cultural mix, as was evidenced in "Edgehill," the guest house I mentioned previously. I recall our British Colonel friend, Alan Norrish, saying plaintively on a beautiful July fourth evening, "I say...would you mind allowing some of our American guests access to the fireworks?" General laughter erupted as the multi-national group realized they were hogging the supplies and enjoying the fun.

Living forty years abroad in the same country certainly provided Allen and me adequate time to work through the four daunting stages of adjustment. I had little or no trouble, and my husband also proved to be an apt learner. He counted on his fingers, sat cross-legged on grass mats with ease, enjoyed Indian food, and picked up Hindi pronunciation with alacrity from our village pundit.

Allen was born in Peabody, Kansas. He saw India for the first time on November 20, 1939, and served there in various capacities until we officially retired in the spring of 1981. He assimilated many Indian thought patterns, such as letting *time* do its perfect work. He much prefers patience to raw nerves! Allen loves India, and I know many others who will readily identify with his story.

My history, however, is somewhat different, for I belong to a "neither-nor species" currently known as "third culture kids." My parents went to India as missionaries in 1913, and I was born in Bhagalpur, North Bihar. During my years in boarding school in Darjeeling, I was dubbed a "mish kid," as were others like me. Later that changed to "m.k.'s" with the current appellation of "t.c.k." which simply means a third culture kid. This encompasses all who have known two or more cultures intimately, and are the products of their past. But in my private thoughts I call myself a hybrid—two dominant strains somehow mingling to make me what Allen calls his "American Indian." Perhaps you laugh! Spelled out more clearly, it means I was born in India, spoke Hindi before English, played with village children from the time I could toddle, and ate Indian food in preference to American. Those traits still persist. I speak Hindi without an accent, love the companionship of Indians, and enjoy hot, spicy foods.

Nor am I alone in this. A select group of us "hybrids" continue to find ourselves at odds with both cultures, yet somehow, we cling to each. This dichotomy can cause great conflict and dissatisfaction for those who haven't learned that a dominating third strand can mute the other two and bring them into a harmonious whole. But one must find the right strand!

I am glad I had godly parents who introduced me early to my Lord Jesus Christ. He has my heart. He is my Savior, my Lord. In him there is no East or West, no male or female, no high or low— but Christ is all, and in all. It is true! In the Lord Jesus, differences merge. I am at peace, simply because he is in control. When I forget and take over the reins, a far different scene emerges. Life gets out of balance, and confusion and fear crowd in. Yes, I have known and lived this experientially, too. Experiences pile up when you have lived as long as have I.

We hybrids know emotional highs and lows, as do all who read this book. Problems intensify when we try to break into new thought patterns. I recall the shock I felt in New Delhi when my husband informed me we would be leaving soon for the United States. Not that we hadn't left for the States before, but this time there would be a difference. We were going to retire there!

No returning to India? But India was my home! How could I ever face adjusting to American life? Just thinking about living in America scared me. The country seemed so advanced, so technically sufficient and power-conscious. A slower lifestyle suited me perfectly, and I wasn't interested in moving to the States except for one particular reason. Our daughter had completed her college course and married. With her husband and two children, she lived in Elizabethtown, Pennsylvania. It was a lovely rural area that we knew from our flying visits on home leave. I wanted to be with Joanne, to experience a little of the lost family life we had suffered during long periods of separation.

Couldn't we go to see our family and return? My husband said no, since our missionary support concluded when we reached the magical age of sixty-five. I wondered rebelliously what made the age of sixty five so pivotal. In India a person is surrounded by family members and cared for until the end. Was America going to be different? Would I fit?

Allen assured me that retiring in the States would have its benefits. He produced brightly colored pictures and articles, sent him by his twin brother, Amos, to prove it. I pored over these, trying to assimilate the fact that soon we would be called "senior citizens" instead of "Auntie" and "Uncle." Were we going to be pushed off, away from the action, to the fringes of life in a retirement center? Was there no other alternative?

Through four decades of missionary service in India we had become "family" members, belonging to beautiful Indian people. How could we leave them? And should we do so, where would we get the money to return periodically? The whole picture seemed bleak.

"Allen," I said, "if you are going to move me ten thousand miles to the other side of the world to something I have not previously experienced, please let me take some of my treasures." I named three specific items—mother's teakwood desk, the little rocking chair Allen had designed and made to my measurements, and the cedar chest he had given me for my engagement gift.

Perhaps he felt he was getting by easily, because he also promised to buy me a piano in America! Somewhat mollified, I began sorting, packing, getting ready for the big move. We left India on May 1, 1981, as planned, stopped in Switzerland with friends, visited others in England, then proceeded on to the States.

Our daughter and family awaited us at the Harrisburg Airport. With them stood several members of a caring church fellowship. They carried a large poster that read, "Welcome home, Allen and Leoda." It had been personally signed by scores of members of the church! A warm feeling surged up within me. Perhaps we could belong after all.

A whirlwind week with our immediate family prefaced our month on the West Coast visiting friends and relatives. But we hurried back because our daughter and husband had rented an apartment for us, and we were eager to see it.

Joanne's letter gave directives. Should we arrive in Elizabethtown before 5:00 in the afternoon, we should get the key from our landlady. Joanne and Herb would come immediately upon returning from work.

With considerable excitement Allen and I walked into our new home on a Wednesday afternoon in mid-July, 1981. The living room held one piece of furniture—a davenport that would open into a double bed. Good! We could sleep on it tonight. The airy eat-in kitchen provided an expansive view over grassy fields and a beautiful flowing stream. Who could ask for more? We liked the table and chairs, and noted on our tour of discovery that not only was the refrigerator filled with food, but also the cupboard in the kitchen. Dishes and cutlery had been supplied. Had our immediate family done this, or were others also involved?

Joanne and Herb told us that the same warm-hearted Christian brothers and sisters who signed the large welcome card had stocked our cupboards and refrigerator. A sense of wonder and thanksgiving welled up inside. How could they know how much this meant personally in our hour of transition? Indeed, that love demonstrated practically lifted me beyond myself. I glimpsed something *big*. It is called Christian compassion.

CHAPTER TWO

TRANSPLANTING
A HYBRID

When my parents, Henry and Katie Smith, went to India in 1913, they traveled by ship. Their journey took seven weeks. At the end of 1939, twenty-six years later, Allen and I traveled to India. We also went by ship, taking much the same route across the Pacific Ocean, and our journey also lasted seven weeks. Due to World War II, all Atlantic sea routes had been forcibly closed, but the Pacific remained open.

Seven weeks seems long, but it provided quality time for a comprehensive introduction to oriental ports and culture. Nowadays we do it by air. Whisking around the world on a jet plane is so economical that we can't afford the ocean cruises now touted as luxury items. You see, values have changed, as has technology's amazing advance. We noticed this particularly in western countries.

To be caught in that variation, as were we in a lifetime of travel between India and America, supplied us with many learning experiences. I recall being briefed on the current use of Chinese money and given the exchange rate before we spent several days in Shanghai in 1939. Nor can I forget the horror of visiting a refugee camp in Hong Kong, where entire families lived on crowded wooden platforms that were barely six by eight feet in measurement! Chaotic traffic patterns in Manila and other large cities made me shudder again. But we loved Singapore's cleanliness and rigid discipline. We still do!

Then came unforgettable India with its millions of men, women, and children spilling over each other in trains, on roads, in bazaars. Old busses, tied together with a wire and prayer, rumbled by. Villagers walked country trails single file, baskets of produce balancing on their heads.

Living in North Bihar, a village area, we soon learned to use oxcarts and I finally took to riding a horse for transportation. Allen very soon bought a bicycle. Nine years later, a youth group in Southern California presented him with a James motorcycle to transport him over those sandy trails. When we eventually graduated to a mission jeep, this seemed outright luxurious!

In 1960 we moved to Delhi, the capital of India. We now entered a city that sprawled fifteen to twenty miles from north to south. My brother and family lived on the opposite side of the city from us, but at last we were motorized. We used our motorcycle (which came with us from Bihar,) auto rickshaws, and busses. These replaced the snail-paced travel we had known.

Twenty years in Delhi and Bangalore, the latter a garden city 1,600 miles to the south, made "modern India" come alive in our expanding store of experiences. Here we found a burgeoning middle class of well-informed citizens. They were politically alert, passionately loved sports, and in business pressed their advantage for getting ahead. Yet they exhibited remarkable hospitality skills, and highly revered their family ties. We liked them. Indians are surely beautiful people!

In mid-1981 we returned once more to the United States—the land of our forefathers—after serving as missionaries to India for almost forty-two years. Now what would we face? Would American life contrast greatly with our patterns? Our home-leave assignments during the last twenty years were of short duration, three months at the most, and packed full with meetings and travel. Now we would live here! Would any of our former experiences aid in making necessary adjustments? I fervently hoped so.

Allen slipped into his old grooves much more easily than I. He rejoiced to locate a "Buckwalter Lane" in nearby Lancaster, Pa. When he saw another Allen Buckwallter in the phone directory, he chuckled, and began to sign his name with his middle initial for

**William and Mary Hoke (left) with the Buckwalters
and a New Delhi pastor and wife.**

identification. Moreover, he found that Lancaster County was full
of Buckwalters! All his life overseas, my husband had painstak-
ingly spelled his last name for others. He wouldn't have to do that
now.

Since Allen's parents, Sam and Susan (Kreider) Buckwalter,
had their roots in central Pennsylvania, he soon located cousins and
an aunt. We attended Aunt Sadie's funeral. She died at 98 years of
age, with hair as black as any teenager's!

In touring Amish country, Allen thrilled to see the general store
in New Holland. He knew his father had come from that area.
Imagination blossomed as he began visualizing a little barefoot
country boy, twisting his toes nervously while clutching a penny.
Allen was sure we must be standing in the same room. Surely the
smiling grocer would have patted little Sam on the head as he gave
him the stick candy or licorice he sought.

Yes, Allen had found his roots, but where were mine? Even
when I learned that cousins lived in the area, it didn't stimulate me
to hunt them up. Being born in India, and living most of my life
overseas, I felt like a stranger here, and dreaded making the first

move. Anyway, my personal experience of America had largely been centered in California where I lived as a teenager with my maternal grandparents, Bishop and Mrs. C.C. Burkholder. This made me consider Southern California as my American base.

However, I have found roots in Pennsylvania since my father came from Harrisburg. With his parents and siblings, Henry Smith moved from the capital of the state to a hamlet some ten miles south, named Grantham. City zoning laws forced Grandpa Smith to relocate his Smith Noodle Factory in a suburban area.

I learned, too, that daddy attended Elizabethtown College, graduating in 1908. He then returned to Grantham to teach in his father's newly-established Messiah Bible School and Missionary Training Home. Almost a century later, Messiah College has long since placed Grantham, Pennsylvania, on the map as a center for quality Christian education. Founded by my paternal grandfather, Bishop S.R. Smith, it proudly bears its motto of "Christ Preeminent."

So, in the college I found roots, but because of spending a lifetime abroad, I lacked a sense of continuity. How thankful we were for the one semester Allen and I spent at Messiah as teachers on our first furlough! We personally tasted collegiate life in this very special place.

But these were merely glimpses of America. In fact, I knew much more about India. In this new setting, a sea of questions made me ask myself repeatedly, "What sort of a country is this? What should I do now? Will it be acceptable in this culture?"

Little matters touched off my confusion. For instance, what should I take to a carry-in-dinner? We didn't have "carry-in-dinners" in India. If we had, the answer would have been easy, since our cook turned out delicious pastries and Indian delicacies, all very acceptable. Here? I sighed when I learned that cakes and pies are more highly prized when they are home-baked. When I took my store-bought pie to a carry-in-dinner, the inevitable happened. Someone asked, "Do you have this recipe? It's simply delicious!"

Imagine my embarrassment! So, what did I do? Out of my experience of adaptation, I hope I managed to smile as I answered, "Sorry, my dears, I don't have the recipe. I do my best baking at Ridgeview!"

It was true! I've never learned to bake pastries or pies. What should I do now without a cook? I went to the best supermarket I knew, bought my pie, and it was good. The ladies laughed at my response and began discussing who bakes for Ridgeview Supermarket. I could have hugged them!

One day our daughter told us that our settling here had eased one question for her. Until then people wondered how she fit into the social order. Yes, they knew she had come from India, but did she have relatives around here? Our coming helped place her into this closely-knit Pennsylvania Dutch family-oriented society, and that mattered.

Several months after our arrival, we had a visitor from the local senior citizens' group. Elections were coming, he said, and they were looking for an additional name to place as nominee for president. The other candidate was an influential person in Elizabethtown. Would Allen allow his name to be used? Likely he would not be chosen, but his being on the ballot would automatically place him on the executive committee as vice president. My husband thought it a good chance to learn the inner workings of this intriguing class to which we now belonged. Suddenly we were caught up in the world of our peers.

Thus we became acquainted with a whole new concept. Monthly meetings advertised bus trips and volunteer community service, and urged attendance at the newly established senior citizens' center. Since we were traveling to mission-related meetings, we found eventually we had neither time nor interest in being "senior citizens," so we began to call ourselves "recycled" rather than "retired."

America's affluence jolted us, too. Just one visit to the supermarket in our town made us realize we were experiencing something unknown to millions overseas. Imagine an entire aisle of only paper products! Another aisle for frozen foods? We could scarcely comprehend, for we had come from a country where staples were often rationed.

We looked around our newly-furnished apartment. We had bought prudently since pennies counted. My piano is a used instrument, but its Baldwin Acrosonic label and tone still delights me. It is better than anything I've played in India, even on my programs over the radio!

Our TV set opened a vast world of variety to us, and we marveled at the choice of channels. Delhi has TV, but in our day, we couldn't afford a TV set. However, our neighbor across the street, newly rich, bought one, and to the dismay of all of us, the family would sit out in the yard each evening with the Delhi TV programs turned up loud enough to shatter our nerves. Night after night we heard Hindi dramas. Since they came on about the time we wanted to sleep, Allen counteracted by playing taped music which we liked! That helped.

In America, we not only owned a TV set, but we had a remarkable number of options and soon learned to utilize the off-button! But the TV became a window to the outside world since we didn't subscribe to any newspaper from Lancaster or Harrisburg. Whereas in Delhi, international news was our daily diet, now we lived in a small circle. Sometimes we longed for shortwave, and Allen would get his time signals from Quebec and his news from the BBC in London! He used our India-made small shortwave set!

Both my husband and I shied away from using a telephone. In a land where personal visits or writing letters takes precedence, telephones had been limited with long waiting lists of applications.

Here, spontaneity became history. We couldn't just drop in on our friends or even our family for a chat whenever we felt like it. Time must be managed, structured, controlled. So we learned to schedule visits and appointments.

We tried to adjust. We forgot afternoon tea, and ate supper at five-thirty instead of having dinner at eight. We learned not to mention missing a house servant.

"Why would you have a servant?" my inquirer would ask in a voice that to me implied I must have been too lazy to do my own housekeeping. Were we being "rich Americans" there and spending God's money on ourselves and our own comforts?

How could I just laugh it off and say sincerely, "People in India all help to support someone less fortunate than themselves in an economy miles below this one. We always felt we were supporting an entire family when we hired a cook." I learned it is wise to leave such subjects alone, not to try to explain. Few seemed to understand. It was as though I was speaking a foreign language to them!

American technology amazed us. Telephones weren't only available, they worked—no squealing, no hum, no need to shout. We enjoyed constant hot and cold running water out of our faucets, nor were we bothered with daily power cuts as is common across all of India. I remembered the inconveniences we suffered.

Both in Delhi and Bangalore we had to live with daily power cuts. Lack of electricity often delayed recording our radio programs. "Shedding," as it is called there, causes considerable inconvenience and trouble, especially in the hot weather. But in America we had a steady flow.

We soon learned to expect everything to work! Our first "snafu" here shocked and dismayed us. (A "snafu" is a military term for "situation normal, all fouled up.") In India we would laugh at the "snafus" that regularly came our way. Both in travel and daily life, plans could easily change because of unexpected incidents or interceptions. We thought we had left them behind.

But we soon met one of significant magnitude. In early 1981, several months prior to our leaving India for retirement, a new person in the Social Security office in the U.S. decreed that our monthly allotments should be sent to India in rupees instead of being banked in our local account in Elizabethtown.

This meant big trouble. Money could enter India freely, but legally it couldn't leave the country. Moreover, our system of writing checks on our American bank account had worked well for over a year.

Unaware of the change in policy, we left India to settle in Pennsylvania, but soon after our arrival, our Social Security checks stopped coming! Where were they? Only one payment arrived in Delhi; the others were intercepted somewhere on the way. Several years of appeal brought the delayed amount back to us here, but for many months we found ourselves without any source of income.

"What sort of a country have I come to?" my mind screamed. "How will we live?" Already I had sensed that whereas in India we were considered as rich among the poor, now we were classed as poor among the rich. In near panic, Allen and I called a moratorium on spending—and learned a big lesson. God's goodness and grace took over! People began to give us vegetables and meat liberally without realizing our dire financial need.

Could it be that a Sovereign Lord had transplanted us to this side of the world, and he was in control? Another blessing also surfaced, but it too tested our faith. We were overjoyed when Far East Broadcasting's directors asked us to continue serving, this time as regional representatives in the northeastern states. But we would be expected to raise our own support, they said. Financially inundated already because of the Social Security fiasco, we could but bow our hearts before our Lord and ask him to take over—and he did.

Mission conferences began to fill our days. We made many new friends in our travels from Connecticut to Washington, D.C. Our knowledge of Americans broadened as we met many mission-minded Christians who had the vision of using radio as we had known it.

We often looked up former India contacts. One such trip took us to the nation's capital where we found dear Delhi friends who had served in the American Embassy. Dan and Ann not only hosted us, but took us to the annual FEBC banquet in Washington. To me, everything seemed elegant, but what I remember most clearly was the shock I felt when the speaker criticized communism while recounting stories of persecution to listeners who persisted in their Christian faith.

My thoughts whirled, and I trembled. How could he speak so freely here in the nation's capital city? Didn't he realize he could be shadowed? I laugh at those fears now, for I had yet to learn that in America we possess freedom of speech, along with many other freedoms. Here we were in the dream world that millions overseas desire to enter! That evening in Washington, D.C., culture shock had me firmly in its grip.

Culture shock became apparent at unexpected times. I was stunned to see replays on TV showing peoples' emotions. Perhaps it was a tear trickling down someone's cheek, or an inadvertent reaction to something said or heard, a look of disappointment or joy. "How terrible!" I would exclaim. In retrospect, I puzzled over why I thought it terrible and realized that in the Orient, a person doesn't permit feelings to show! It isn't considered good taste. But in this country, the media plays and replays scenes showing emotion. To me, a "foreigner," this seemed rude. It seemed an infringement on a person's privacy—a perspective that was no doubt very "Indian."

When attending a ladies' luncheon in Pittsburgh, a warm and welcoming atmosphere greeted me, but I remained an observer. I felt totally out of the action, not included. I simply didn't belong. Was something wrong with me?

For a long time I puzzled over my reaction, until it dawned on me that in India, women seldom did anything apart from other family members—except perhaps to go to a religious fair or on a pilgrimage. Womens' Rights movements might be in vogue in the New India, but I hadn't encountered them since we constantly lived within the context of a more conservative community or church group. I was suffering culture shock.

One evening in St. Petersburg, Florida, I felt completely out of place. Friends had invited us to a sacred concert. Arriving before the auditorium doors opened on that balmy evening, we waited outside, as did hundreds of others who also desired a good seat. I looked around and wondered what we were doing here—everyone had grey hair or white! But my second thoughts made me smile. I, too, had silvery white hair since my fifties, when two months of fever laid me low. By now, white hair shouldn't bother me. Why should I feel out of place?

Thinking it through, it became clear to me that this situation was unique in that these were all senior citizens. In India we don't have such gatherings. Young people congregate for their conferences, and rallies are held where all ages attend. But there is no separate senior citizens' class! There are several retirement homes in Bangalore, established during our time, and sponsored by a local Christian church to aid those of their congregation who needed such care. But I don't remember ever being surrounded before by hundreds of senior citizens, and I was suffering culture shock.

Mine wasn't a serious case, for which I am thankful. Culture shock can bring on many attending symptoms—physically, emotionally, and mentally. Loss of appetite and sleep are common. Loss of interest in the new locale can turn into a severe bout of homesickness so great that the individual suffers poor concentration. Fatigue takes over, and this leads to refusing responsibilities due to feelings of insecurity. A record in one's mind plays over and

over again, "I've goofed. I can't handle this. I want to go home!"
At that point the person often does go home, like one of our house
guests did in Delhi.

We had prepared for his coming from the States, and felt privi-
leged to entertain him since he was one of the speakers in an
international meeting. He arrived on time. Sick from some virus
that he caught in his visit to Nepal prior to coming to us, he barely stayed one day! Culture shock laid him so low emotionally that
he canceled all engagements and caught the first flight back to the
States. He wanted his own doctor! He trusted none other, even
though his symptoms seemed ordinary to us. He couldn't take any
more, even though he was the editor of a well-known magazine.

As mentioned, I suffered culture shock during our first eighteen
months in the States, but thankfully, I never gave in to the nagging
refrain, "I can't handle this, I want to go home." The saving feature
may have been our work with mission-minded people. We felt it to
be an extension of our years of service in missionary radio in India,
and we greatly enjoyed every contact.

However, we did return to India sooner than planned. When
our bank account in Delhi suddenly burgeoned with the unexpected arrival of our Social Security allotment, it was also jeopardized.
The money couldn't be returned, so dear Lawrence (with power of
attorney) was harassed by a demand for taxes in the name of Mis-
ter L. Buckwalter, c/o Centenary Church, New Delhi. He had to
pay. Much distressed, he wrote us immediately. After prayerful con-
sideration, we knew we must close out the account, so we returned
to spend the rest of the money within the country.

Our visit felt like a reunion after an elongated home leave. We
traveled widely by train, visiting friends and places we loved. A
memorable week following Christmas was spent in a mountain
setting with my brother and family. Housebound due to a five-
inch snowfall, we learned to know each other very well, a truly
beautiful experience!

In early January 1983, we attended the annual convention of the
Evangelical Fellowship of India (EFI). This week-long meeting
convened in Agra, 120 miles south of Delhi. Agra is primarily
known for its world-famous Taj Mahal.

For almost twenty years prior to retirement, I had served as EFI's official pianist. When the Indian leadership heard we were in India again, they immediately asked Allen to be music director and wanted me at the piano. We consented.

Instead of taking an auditorium as the site for the convention, the committee erected a large canvas tent on the campus of a Christian school. Last-minute preparations were proceeding when we arrived during the early afternoon of the day the meetings would begin. The workers had completed the speakers' platform, but one for the piano remained to be erected. With true Indian ingenuity, men accomplished this within minutes by placing two wooden beds side by side! We wondered whether it would hold both an upright piano and a chair. We would soon find out.

The piano arrived on a manually-drawn cycle rickshaw about an hour before service began. We were startled, but then, this was India, not America! Several men hoisted the instrument onto the platform and placed a chair for my convenience. Allen checked everything. Deciding that I would need a step to help me mount easily, he soon laid some burned bricks in position which he found in the corner of the compound. Meanwhile, our helper brought two more chairs for our personal use during the service, and we were ready.

A large crowd attended the opening service. In true Indian fashion, welcome speeches and music items followed each other. The piano sounded fairly good to me, but I longed for my Baldwin Acrosonic! However, the excellent message by a nationally-known Indian evangelist made us sure we were in for an exceptional week.

The next morning, several hundred delegates met for Bible study. Allen and I were seated as usual near the piano. When the speaker began his concluding prayer, I climbed the steps to prepare for the closing hymn.

But when I attempted to sit down, the chair under me slipped backwards with me on it! Allen heard a crunch. He looked up, then jumped to rescue me from a fall. But there I lay, as in a hammock, held up by the canvas wall behind me. He struggled to pull me up with both hands, but nothing budged! The evangelist kept on praying.

John Richard, our Indian brother who was the EFI General Secretary, looked up, then moved fast. He took one of my hands while Allen pulled the other, and between them, thank God, they rescued this lady in distress—while the evangelist prayed on!

Almost bursting inside with the ridiculous situation in which I found myself, I tried not to laugh aloud. Fortunately the piano was an upright instead of a baby grand. I hoped it hid me from the audience, who customarily bowed their heads and closed their eyes in prayer.

When the "Amen" finally came, John Richard hastily gave a benediction, and immediately sent some men for another bed to enlarge the piano platform. The crisis had passed. All was well, and I thanked God I suffered no ill effects from the incident.

But when Allen and I were alone in our hotel room, I burst into laughter. He seemed surprised. He saw the fall quite differently than did I, and fervently rejoiced that I wasn't in the hospital with a broken back or neck.

Surely the Lord graciously preserved me that day, but in retrospect, I puzzled over my reaction. In India I was able to "take it" and laughed. Was it due to my having returned "home"? I thought back over the past eighteen months in a new setting. Much smaller incidents had placed stress and near panic upon me. If God could preserve me in India and keep me from falling, wouldn't he take care of me in America also? Why did I doubt? Couldn't I trust?

I could—but I would have to change focus. Trusting demands looking at the Savior rather than the circumstances, or at my feelings. It was time for me to relearn that lesson.

CHAPTER THREE

WHAT SORT OF COUNTRY HAVE I COME TO?

My husband and I have always enjoyed plants. Here in America we have found satisfaction in cultivating some beautiful house plants that we never had in India. We have a number of spider plants, several varieties of African violets, and a Christmas cactus. I want to tell you about the latter.

We knew that any type of cactus has its natural habitat in desert country. By no stretch of imagination could Lancaster County qualify! But Allen and I lived our teenage years in Southern California and we learned to love the vast open spaces of desert and mountains that the West affords. So we nurtured our little Christmas cactus, wondering whether it could survive even in our sunniest window.

It came to us as a gift and bloomed profusely twice a year. Each time I laughed with amazement. Whoever heard of a flower coming out of its leaf? Not only that, but this is a plant that does things differently from the norm. Not only does it shoot one flower out of the end of the leaf, but as if to shout "Victory," it sends a beautiful blossom out of the first! I decided the Lord used not only ingenuity but humor when he created this variety of cactus.

And it bloomed twice a year. We were used to yucca plants, found in desert areas of the High Sierras. Their blooms come only after many years and cause tremendous interest. As young people, we thought nothing of driving to the desert to see the wild flowers,

Our Christmas cactus.

including yuccas in bloom. They were often called "The Lord's Candle."

So, our little cactus bloomed twice a year regularly for us. Allen photographed it, and visitors exclaimed over its beauty. But one day we looked at each other and said, "It needs a larger pot. It must be root-bound in that container."

Allen found a pretty, light green ceramic flower pot and transplanted it. He set it in the patio where it would get maximum sunlight. It grew profusely, and we looked for it to bloom at the usual time. The plant appeared to be coping well. But something had gone wrong. Although healthy looking, no blooms came at Thanksgiving and Easter as formerly. Instead, some buds appeared around Christmas time. Was the plant disoriented?

Another difference became apparent. These new blooms weren't hardy as the former ones had been. They withered and fell after a day or two. Much distressed, we are still wondering whether our transplanted "hybrid" is going to make it.

That's what I asked myself when I found American "soil" and "climate" so completely foreign to anything I had known from my childhood. Where were family values? Where was true interest in keeping God's laws? In India even the Muslims observed a high code of ethics. I was beginning to sense that here, many people lived in a murky grey zone instead of black or white.

My first eighteen months after retirement in America were certainly haphazardly disoriented. Perhaps outwardly I appeared calm, doing well. I truly did try to adapt to my new circumstances, but inwardly I sought answers to all the questions that kept harassing me. Foremost was, "What sort of a country have I come to?"

Actually, I began wrestling with this question several years earlier when, in 1979, Allen and I transferred from Bangalore, South India, to India's capital city, New Delhi, some 1,600 miles northward. Allen had just handed over the FEBA India's directorship to an Indian brother, and we hoped we could take a short furlough, then return to our new place of work. But it turned out that Allen had to move our belongings during the month (which for me elongated to two) of "compassion leave." This was granted by the Mission Board under which we served. I felt I must see my 96-year-old stepfather in April. Mother had died years before, when we were in India. Now I wanted to see Daddy Harry, so I came alone to the States.

Our daughter and family lived in Elizabethtown. They drove to the airport in Philadelphia to meet me. As soon as I met my family, Joanne said, "Mother, I'm sorry, but I have bad news for you. Uncle Amos has been seriously injured in a car accident and is hospitalized in Kirkland Lake in Canada."

Amos was Allen's twin! I must go to him if at all possible. I must do it for my husband, and the missions office helped me find a ride the next afternoon with a Canadian pastor and his wife. Two days later my sister-in-law met me in Southern Ontario, and I arrived in Kirkland Lake, 500 miles north of Toronto, by late that night.

As we entered the parsonage, the telephone rang. Our daughter, Joanne, had called and now said, "Mother, I've been trying to get you! Everybody here has been warned that we might have to evacuate because of an accident at Three Mile Island. Don't come home until you hear from me."

I could scarcely comprehend. She explained that TMI was a nuclear plant only eight miles away. All in the area had been told to prepare for evacuation. In fact, many were already leaving their homes. We would keep in touch.

I remained calm outwardly, but inwardly my tired body and mind screamed, "What sort of a country have I come to?" A restful week with Alice did much to restore me. We visited Amos daily and were pleased to note his improvement. Then I returned to Southern Ontario, this time by train. It would be an overnight journey with an onward connection to Niagara Falls from Toronto. It didn't happen as planned.

Just north of the city, a motorist ran squarely into our moving train, hitting the compartment in which I was sitting. All of us felt a terrible jolt, but the train kept on going. By the time it stopped, backed up, and all details were cleared, I knew I was in for serious trouble in Toronto. I had missed my connection.

What should I do? What does one do in a case like this? I asked a kindly-looking porter and he replied, "Ma'am, just tell the first person in uniform when we stop." With that directive, I joined the throng of purposeful people streaming through the immense Toronto station. Lugging my heavy suitcase, I said breathlessly to a man calling the number of a train, "Please, sir, I've missed mine to Niagara Falls because of an accident." I hoped I'd said the right thing.

He took his walkie-talkie (something I didn't recognize since I'd never seen one before) and talked with the station master. "He wants to see you personally," my informant said and gave me directions. I felt a sinking feeling in my stomach, but managed to find the right office. When I told my story, compassion such as I'd seldom experienced poured out. "We'll take care of you, ma'am," my new friend said, and he kept his word. He phoned my friends, told them when and where to meet me, then had someone carry my suitcase to my waiting train. It had been held fully a half-hour because of me!

Bewildered, hungry, and confused, I sank gratefully onto a seat. Simultaneously we started moving. Passengers around me were complaining at the delay. "It's never late," they said, but it was today, and I was the cause. Or was I? At that point I asked myself wearily again, "What sort of a country have I come to?"

The driver of the automobile that crashed into our moving railroad car was instantly killed. Some wondered if he had tried to commit suicide. His fellow passenger was seriously injured. We learned they were on their way to a nearby factory, but never made it. That's sobering!

But this particularly prickly beginning turned out well for me. My friends met me at the right station at the time appointed. Joanne and Herb and family never did have to evacuate their home, but for days they kept an emergency kit in the back of their car, ready to go on a moment's notice.

When I finally returned to Pennsylvania, all was again quiet, and life fell into normal routines. I went to California, spent quality time with Daddy Harry and several aunts and uncles. Three weeks later, the Lord took my stepfather home. I had gone to America at the right time!

Two years later, when Allen and I retired from service in India and returned to America, the same sort of haphazard living day by day took over again. I was still an observer. American life unfolded around me. It seemed different, often unique, always intriguing. It was a world apart from the culture with which I had become so familiar. This was definitely "foreign."

We had come from a country where religious faith marks everyone, regardless of which deity each one follows. Because I was a returned missionary, I think I expected to find a virile Christian faith in this so-called Christian land. I saw outward trappings of Christianity boldly displayed: a dozen churches in our small town advertised their Sunday services and other functions in the local newspaper, and two Christian radio stations, each catering to a segment of society, so we even had options! Contrastingly, we soon learned that not all so-called "Christians" even go to church!

Our neighbor next door said she went to church regularly, but her husband found he had to take one day of rest because of his exhausting work. That sounded strange, since I had come from a land where the temple bells begin tolling in the early morning hours, calling on worshippers and deities alike. And the Hindus go! How early? At four-thirty in the morning.

What about the Muslims? The devout begin their prayer vigils when they hear the first call of the *Mulvi* intoning over a loud speaker, "There is one God, Allah, and Mohammed is his prophet." I have seen Muslims spread their prayer mats in trains, on busy sidewalks, and other public places when the time for prayer comes. I began to wonder whether people here aren't challenged to a living faith.

Perhaps we needed role models who would fearlessly live their devotion. I recall attending a convention for Christian young people in Bhubaneshwar, Orissa, about two hundred miles south of Calcutta. Those vibrant youth leaders exuded joy and confidence because they had seen their pastors go to prison for their faith. They knew that they, too, were in the mark, yet they were ready to go if and when the opportunity came. These youth leaders had good role models to follow! Could Christians in the West learn from them? I asked myself, to whom do we belong, anyway? Are we Christ's, or aren't we? Whose good are we seeking? Whose glory?

The majoring on minor or secondary issues here bothered me, too. We soon learned that theological differences were considered far more important among denominations in our present locale than they had been in India. There, confronted with Hinduism, Islam, and spirit worshipers, plus many other facets of Eastern mysticism, Christians worked together wholeheartedly. In all my work in public relations for FEBA India, I had never been asked to submit a statement concerning my personal stand on controversial issues. Presenting our official FEBC Statement of Faith always sufficed.

Yet, in our travels to missions' conferences here, at times we were asked to identify our personal stand on some prickly issues that to us, as missionaries, really held little meaning! If we gave the "right" answer, we could be expected back; if not, then FEBC was bypassed for some other organization. This is America!

Radio commercials annoyed us constantly. Allen hasn't made peace with them yet. He relishes the "off button" on both TV and radio, a habit likely shared by millions of other listeners. But the use of air time for raising funds on religious programs seemed even worse. If they were honoring God, wouldn't he supply their need? I knew he would, because for twenty years in FEBA India, we watched this happen month after month. Yet none of our programs ever mentioned money. It was taboo!

How then did we manage? By praying for our needs to be met, and watching the Lord answer those prayers! Each day's mail brought in letters from listeners. Many contained offerings. Cash money orders arrived daily, too. A note on the bottom of the money order often revealed the motivation. Letters also told the secret, and it was always the Lord who had blessed the listener through the program. God got the glory.

To thank donors, I trained my staff to write personal letters. When the management decreed a printed card, saying it would save time, I knew they were on the wrong track. Someone who has received spiritual blessing from God and sends an offering to a worthy cause in his name deserves a personal word. We sent out the printed card, but on the back I wrote a personal note. When we were moved from Delhi to Bangalore headquarters, the donors sent their gifts to me there. They wanted to be thanked personally!

We formed a prayer fellowship of Christian listeners. Each member signed a declaration of faith in Jesus Christ, and many became loyal supporters. The count of members in India totaled 8,000 when we left in 1981. By 1990, the number had grown to 12,500 members. How does FEBA India do this? By the personal touch, both by letter and local radio rallies. Sometimes "Christian America" seems a world away from what we knew in India.

Nevertheless, I marvel at this country's reaching out to people in need. A lost child gains nation-wide attention, with great rejoicing when he is found and restored to his anxious family. Catastrophes gain national coverage, understandably, but the attending response is unique. Volunteers spring into action, pocket books are opened, and all age groups participate in trying to rebuild and aid. Christian compassion is definitely shown here, and we marvel.

I believe spiritual hunger is also here. Down through this century, Dr. Billy Graham has fearlessly preached the gospel with integrity and purpose. The Spirit of God brings not hundreds, but thousands to seek and find. Lives are changed, and God gets the glory.

Megachurches have become part of the national scene. At the end of this millennium, there is a renewed thrust for the souls of men, women, and children. Even while crime increases and commitment to Jesus Christ seems outmoded and outdated, yet the

Spirit of God continues drawing people back to the biblical faith of their fathers. God is faithful.

At the same time, the force of Eastern mysticism is also being felt in every strata of society. A friend of mine shared the religion section of a Harrisburg newspaper with us. We found the news items, articles, and notices of great interest. One day as I read an open letter, I suddenly realized that pure, undisguised Hinduism was pouring forth! My eyes were opened, and I began a new quest. How far had this penetrated into American thought, life, and practice?

I remembered the 1960s in India, when a trickle of young people seeking peace arrived in Delhi to get their visas renewed. We lived there at that time, and one day a girl from Australia, who had been intercepted by wide-awake missionaries, stood on our doorstep. She had been to Bali, Thailand, and Nepal—all in search of soul peace. Now she found it in Jesus Christ!

The trickle became a flood of westerners interested in espousing or investigating Eastern mysticism. I recall a Hare Krishna conference held in a large open tent in the very heart of New Delhi. Loud speakers blared forth. Foreigners attended by the planeload. We happened to go to the airport to meet our niece coming from America. While waiting for her plane in the early morning, one of these chartered flights for the conference arrived. Amazed, we watched hundreds of well-dressed Europeans come through those doors to be cleared through customs. What had happened to Europe?

Hippies renewed their tourist visas in Delhi. Unfortunately, most of them likely met with rough treatment, for the Indian mind simply couldn't conceive of any westerner voluntarily renouncing the affluence of the West to seek the spirituality of the East.

Not for long, though! The astute caught on quickly that here was a ready-made market for export! Westerners wanted what Hinduism had to offer! So prominent advertisements began to appear in Delhi newspapers, asking for gurus to go to Western countries to teach Hinduism. That began the march of *swamis* and *maharishis* to this and other lands. Its results are common knowledge.

India has well been called the "mother of religions." A converted Brahman in Delhi, K. V. Pillai, whom we knew well, has written a thought-provoking book entitled, *India's Search for the Unknown Christ*. I treasure our copy.

In it he says that for thousands of years, Indian philosophers have attempted to go beyond this material world, and all that is passing away. Hinduism considers things as unreal, an illusion which they call "maya." This concept has great repercussions—an alternative to biblical concepts, if you please. All is illusion, so the mores vanish, sin and guilt go out the window, and a savior isn't needed after all. We can do it ourselves! Very attractive, indeed!

I wanted to be sure, so I subscribed to a New Age magazine to see what it actually offered to the American mind. I learned a lot.

One observation became very clear. The New Agers have influenced millions by changing the meaning of well-known words such as "spirituality." Their teachings have systematically invaded every part of secular life, so that thought patterns are changing. I have found clues in education, medical techniques, and business. One day a friend said to me, "I think I'll take some yoga classes. It will be good for my health."

Where does yoga come from? India! It is an integral part of Hinduism. So are beliefs in reincarnation, fate, astrology, and being one with "mother nature." Does this sound familiar? Even while many do not suspect its dangers, there are some New Age leaders (now termed the New Spirituality) who have discovered an aching void that only Jesus Christ can fill. It is good to listen to those who can speak personally.

Paul Pillai is one of them. Paul, a converted Brahman, established a Bible school in Delhi, India. He wrote a book as required curriculum for the pastoral course. He goes deep into Indian thought and searchings, and shows that Jesus Christ is the answer.

In giving his testimony, Paul says he would never have come to the Lord through argument or discussion. But when he was sick and needed a friend, a Christian brother came to his bedside and prayed for his healing in the name of Jesus. He was instantly healed! That miracle showed him that Jesus Christ has power. His advice to young seminarians is to stay away from argument and just let Jesus Christ be Lord!

I am reminded of an experience we had in Delhi shortly after moving from North Bihar. Our first Christmas in the city afforded us the opportunity to invite our neighbors in for a Christmas tea. Sandwiched in between two Hindu families, we were thrilled when they accepted our invitation.

Mr. Lumba, an engineer who went out on jobs quite often, lived in the first floor apartment with his wife and daughter. Not long into the afternoon, he came over to where I was serving tea and started a conversation. I considered this very unusual, because in village India (where we had lived for the preceding twenty years) men and women were much more segregated than in urban Delhi.

Mr. Lumba said something like this, as clearly as I can recall: "Mrs. Buckwalter, you are an American. I understand that one of our great teachers, Sadhu Vivekanand, found a warm reception in your country. That's very good, because all religions lead to God."

I remarked, "You're right, Mr. Lumba. The *sadhu* was much appreciated in his meetings in Chicago. But I don't class Christianity as a religion. It is different from the others."

He must have been enjoying the conversation because he asked, "Why not? I understand that America is very religious."

"Maybe so, but I don't class Christianity as a religion for one reason. Religions reach up toward God. In Christianity we find God reaching down for man. He sent Jesus Christ."

The engineer paused, then answered, "You are speaking on a very high philosophical plane."

"Not at all, friend. It's a matter of history. You see, Christianity is Christ. Take him away, and all you have left are some nice ethics." Mr. Lumba was listening, so I continued, "And if Christ died and rose again, as the Scriptures claim, then one should be able to meet him. I have done so, and he has changed my life."

"Humph! It's men who have spiritual experiences!"

"Quite right, again. Men do have spiritual experiences. But my Jesus Christ is different from all others, in that he accepts not only men, but also women, and children. Why, Mr. Lumba, he took the children up in his arms and blessed them." The gentleman turned around abruptly, called his wife and daughter and said, "It's time to go home."

As they left my heart sank. Had we lost them as friends? But the next time the engineer went out on tour, he said to his wife (who told me), "Stay close to Mr. and Mrs. Buckwalter. They know God!"

We can't go wrong when we present Jesus Christ clearly and let him draw people to himself. I had learned that lesson in India. It was time to relearn it in America, too. At the end of three years of searching and asking questions, I began to find my answer. It was a new revelation of my Lord. My heart rejoiced. With hope springing up within, I began to believe that this transplant, too, could survive and bloom where it was planted.

CHAPTER FOUR

SOMETHING SPECIAL
IN SEPTEMBER

I don't remember where we went nor what we did on New Year's Day of 1984. January 1, 1984, stands out as unforgettable for one single reason—in my devotions that morning the Lord spoke clearly and said that something special would happen in September.

Like a child, I was filled with excitement. As though I stood on tiptoe, I looked over the coming year, trying to guess what it might be. One thing I knew. As a gift from the Lord's own hand, it would be good. Maybe God would allow me to return to India, I thought wistfully. When news of a tour party of former students from my Darjeeling days reached me, I was sure this must be it. And when Allen told me on the morning of my birthday that he was sending me with the school party on that India tour, I laughed for joy.

It didn't take me long to send in my reservation and down payment. We were booked on September 7, to spend several weeks in the land I loved so dearly. I anticipated September.

That spring we faced another full schedule of mission conferences. One such appointment took my husband to Williamsburg, Virginia. I stayed home. On his return he talked excitedly about his experiences, his host family, and the sightseeing he did between meetings. He added, "Leoda, you should have gone along. I'm going to take you there. It will give you a real sense of colonial times."

Hmmm, I thought, so you think I should learn some American history? Of course I do need to know more about this land of my forefathers, but why do you suggest it now? I'm currently interested more in India than America. It's sort of like you asking me to eat cooked turnips instead of raw ones which I prefer. Aren't we allowed to have our own preferences?

My thoughts went on and on, but the Lord knew that Allen was right, and I was wrong. Not too long afterwards, my husband took me to Williamsburg, Virginia, for what proved to be a pivotal experience. I chose there to become an American!

The day began by our seeing a movie in the information center. As it vividly recreated history, something happened to me. I felt I could identify. These early settlers were strong men and women who voluntarily faced the challenge of a new world. Here they hoped to carve out a new life for themselves and posterity. Yet they maintained personal loyalties to Britain's king, and no doubt, those ties were precious.

However, the day came when they had to choose. Would they remain loyalists, or cast their lot with the emerging colonies who now sought independence from the Crown? They knew full well the cost of such action. In identifying with the new nation, they would divorce themselves from their past. But their strength would merge with other colonists to bolster this new United States of America. It was truly a great moment in history.

My personal situation confronted me. I, too, had to choose—not between Jesus Christ and America, for he crosses all boundaries. I knew I belonged to him. My choice now had to do with my willingness to identify completely with this land of opportunity, challenge, and problems!

One fact stabilized me. My loving heavenly Father had transplanted me here. Our recent trip to India confirmed this, for the empty spots we left had been filled. Could I now cut ties with India to become one with these to whom we now ministered? Would I choose to become an American? All my life I had carried an American passport, but deep inside, emotionally I belonged to India. Now I must choose.

My attitudes changed that day. I decided to become a participant instead of remaining an observer in a strange land. Looking back, I can now see that a loving Lord was understanding my thoughts and motives, and he was merely preparing me for September. Many

Allen and Leoda with their daughter and son-in-law, Joanne and Herb High, and their children, David and Shana.

times I wondered about the Lord's promise to me about September. How would Williamsburg fit into the picture?

In May 1984, we entertained a very special guest in our two-bedroom apartment. A surprise visit brought us our FEBA India office manager from Bangalore. On his first time out of his homeland, he now came to visit relatives in New York City who had paid his way. Johnny was like a member of our family. For five glorious days we shared deeply together.

But Johnny didn't like Western cuisine, so I cooked Indian food. It seemed like a grand finale to my being Indian rather than American! But September was coming.

In June, just before leaving on another missions tour—this time to New York State and other points—Allen and I got a telephone call from our daughter and son-in-law. That shaped the form of our days ahead. Our family wanted to know whether we were tired of renting and would be interested in helping to buy a home in or around Elizabethtown. They had seen something suitable and wanted to show it to us.

We met their agent who showed us many homes for sale, but the only one that really caught our attention was the one Joanne and

Herb had seen. We decided to take a risk financially, if need be, for we would have to take a loan. Several weeks later, we did give the down payment and the house went into escrow while we continued our tour.

This was in June. The school party was leaving for India in September. Now my new attitude began to show, as I reconsidered spending money on a trip when we needed it for a home. As a result, I canceled my reservation, and decided the Lord was giving us a house in September.

But we ran into another big "snafu" (situation normal, all fouled up!). Nothing was working out—we couldn't get a loan, and the couple who had initially stated they would help us changed their minds. All of this when the house was already in escrow! Besides, we had a number of appointments to fill for FEBC, so we would be out of town until near the time for the final settlement. Where could we find someone to take joint ownership with us?

Of course we prayed. People usually do when they get in trouble. What we failed to see was that this thorny path didn't necessarily mean we were out of the will of God. He was right with us, each step of the way. But he was letting the situation become so muddled that when he stepped in, we would give him the glory! That's very often the pattern. We should know by now, for we have proven him faithful in our walking by faith over the years, both in India and here.

The Lord *was* in control, even when we couldn't see any way out. So it seemed extremely providential to us when the real estate agent through whom we were working decided to take the joint ownership we needed. Being Christians, he and his wife desired these missionaries to have a home of their own.

We received their offer, and the paper signed with their signatures, while we were in Virginia. All Allen and I needed to do was to cosign it. However, we waited. Our next appointment in Ohio would end our engagements, so we expected to return home within the week. We decided to wait until we got to Pennsylvania to pursue the matter.

Through the entire summer, Allen still held some reservations in his heart concerning this particular house. Possibly this helped deter us from cosigning anything. After finishing our last service in

Allen and Leoda's home for twelve years in Elizabethtown.

eastern Ohio, we went to our host's home and received a phone call from Joanne. When I took the phone she asked, "Mother, have you signed anything?"

"No, dear," I answered. "Daddy and I received the paper in Virginia, but we decided to wait until we get home. We come tomorrow, you know."

"Mother! Don't sign! We've found the cutest little house, a single unit. It's up for sale, but hasn't gone on the market yet. Friends of ours told us about it, and we saw it this evening. It has your name written all over it."

We could scarcely sleep for excitement. The Lord had obviously stepped in! A hard day's travel brought us into Elizabethtown by 10:00 on Monday night, but regardless of time, we drove past the little cottage on East Willow Street. We loved its stone front exterior. It looked English.

Going through it the next day confirmed our first impressions. It suited us perfectly, and our family came to our financial aid. We have never doubted this to be the place the Lord chose for us, and we are very grateful. We moved in by mid-October, so what was the Lord's surprise for me in September? Had I been imagining things?

On September 1, 1984, I felt a surging of words within with a mandate to write them down. I went to my typewriter and started. The sentences flowed, and soon I was deep in a book-length manuscript that I captioned, "The House the Storm Built." Unless attending church, I wrote every day, and completed the first draft on the last day of the month. The story recounted the events of our second term. Much of the material is now in the book called *The Chief's Son.*

Meanwhile, Allen packed furiously, recognizing that he would get no help from me. I was as one possessed, needing to put onto paper that which I felt in my heart.

The urge to write, the motivation to do it for his glory, was the gift God gave me. It has been there ever since. I don't believe the Lord handed out any special talent, or inspired words. True, I compose on the typewriter, but my first three drafts are simply not fit for publication. In these twelve years of writing and rewriting, however, eight books have been published, all but one by Evangel Publishing House. We self-published *Window Seat on a Crowded Train.*

Actually, Allen wrote the first book published out of the seven, and I did the rest. I also did the final rewrite and editing on my husband's book. The urge to write has been God's gift, and it began in September 1984.

My brother and sister-in-law, Joe and Marietta Smith, who had spent over thirty years in India, came to stay with us prior to their returning for their final term of service. This was a little over a month after we moved into our new home. Marietta spent much of her ten days reading my manuscript, slashing it with her red pen! Syntax, grammar, sentence construction came under her scrutiny, as well as content. She seemed ruthless to me, for I was still tasting the euphoria that accompanied my completing this mammoth task. Now I realized it was not a completed work, but only the first draft. I would have to learn my skill!

After they left, with a fire burning inside of me to write, I walked to the Christian book store in town and ordered what I wanted for Christmas—two books entitled *Teach Yourself to Write* and *Writing to Inspire.* Having done so, I said to Allen with a satisfied air as I presented the bill, "Thanks for my Christmas present. This is what I want!"

That began my serious study of writing. Subscribing to a nationally-known writers' magazine taught me much, and later I took a two-year correspondence course in novel and short story writing. I completed it in one year's time. All this while I was constantly seeking my genre, my target group, and the content the Lord would have me share with others. Was I to write for children? Young adults? Women only? Bible teaching? Stories? Was it to be articles for magazines or was I to write books? Meanwhile I built up a nice library by joining a writers' book club, and I soon learned that these "how to" books agreed unanimously on one thing. I should write concerning that which I know best.

The answer was obvious. Whenever the Lord moved me to write a major work, "India" came out. Was anyone interested in India? So little news filtered through in the papers or on the media. Yet, when I noted the number of specials on TV that portrayed Indian life and culture, it seemed obvious that a much larger segment of American society than publishers suspected was truly interested in that great subcontinent.

Mysticism from the East was surely impacting American culture. Why wouldn't there be a market for books about India? So, let me try. *Silhouette: Colonial India as We Lived It* began to flow. Evangel Publishing House released it in 1988, just a year after Allen had a stroke.

The stroke hit his speech and swallowing and hospitalized him for one month. During those stress-filled days, I spent the early morning hours writing. Afternoons and evenings were given to being with my husband in the hospital. Thus the motivation to write, always strong, became a source of great blessing to me in coping with outward circumstances. I thank the Lord.

Silhouette tells the story of our first term of eight years in India. How could I trust my memory? How could I reconstruct it as though it happened yesterday, even as that movie in Williamsburg did that so radically changed me?

The Lord took care of that, too. Allen's parents preserved all his correspondence. He dutifully wrote almost every week, much of it in detail. Many times he drew diagrams to clarify something of particular interest. When we settled in Elizabethtown, all those letters came back to us! With such potent reminders, the story took shape.

And before it ever left the house, my husband scrutinized every page. He has the right of veto!

Reading those letters, written when it happened, our memories came alive. I began to write creative non-fiction, and later, two books of fiction. All have been set in India, the land I know best.

After writing *The Chief's Son*, my second book, it went to the publisher, as had the first. He asked an editor friend to read it and critique it, and she slashed it for one particular fault. The story line was good, she said, but it was one dimensional!

To me this was a gigantic "snafu." What does one-dimensional mean when speaking about a manuscript? Our publisher came and talked it over one day, and then I understood. What the story needed was depth! I had told the details, but in America that isn't enough. A sated TV listenership is constantly treated to tear-jerking, threatening situations that stir the emotions. Only then is it good.

Could I do that, he asked? Could I try?

Yes, I could try, but I was up against a stone wall, since orientals ordinarily don't like to show their feelings. Much of the time it seems like they are wearing a mask. You don't know what they are really thinking. Such thoughts raced through my mind before I answered.

"Yes, I can try," I responded slowly. "But with the main characters of the story ten thousand miles away, and no chance to interview them or get their viewpoint, there's only one way I see to do it." I paused, then continued, "By looking deep into my own heart, I can give this a complete overhaul, and just hope that people on the other side of the world feel inwardly as we do."

He smiled, and told me to go ahead. The story that evolved has been termed by some as my best!

My husband has the gift of helping others, and he had habitually put it to good use in any and every situation in India. Before I began to write, I did the cooking. Allen took the lead in our work as North Eastern representatives for Far East Broadcasting; my job was to be a true helper. But several interesting facts surfaced.

The first was that he didn't relish preaching. He believed in it and preached when asked, but when the stroke took him off the public platform, his God-given gift for helping others in need proved a life-saver.

One day we took one of my manuscripts to the missions office for perusal. My interviewer looked it over, then asked, "Do you enjoy writing, Leoda?"

"Oh, yes," I replied, "but one thing bothers me."

He looked up with interest, the papers in his hand, and asked, "And what is that?"

"Well," I said, "when I'm writing, and the words are flowing, suddenly I look at the clock. It's eleven-thirty, time for me to get lunch. I have to go and cook, you know."

He chuckled, then turned to Allen and said with a smile, "If she's writing your story, you should be able to make her lunch."

I didn't forget! Moreover, Allen soon learned that he enjoyed this new task. Now he takes pride in his cooking. Being competitive in nature, he enjoys a challenge. Casseroles held his interest recently; nowadays it is curries.

We opened an FEBC regional office several months after our move in 1984. President Bob Bowman, co-founder of FEBC, cut the ribbon and officiated at the victory banquet on a wintry February night. Coming as it did just prior to the National Religious Broadcasters' meeting in Washington, D.C., we were pleased to have several more members of the headquarters' staff with us.

For three years Allen and I carried the load of office duties, sharing responsibilities. He handled official correspondence, spoke at meetings, and did all the driving and travel arrangements. I maintained daily office routines, attending as many conferences with my husband as possible.

The stroke changed this entire picture. It took Allen off the platform and placed him in the pew. Although he regained many of his former skills, now he used me as his spokesman.

When we visited India three years later, we wrote ahead informing all concerned that Allen wouldn't be able to preach. But when we went, from the day of arrival our friends simply wouldn't permit "Uncle Buckwalter" to remain silent. Time after time my husband would begin speaking to crowds, but after several minutes his voice would give out. Then, with a wry smile he would turn to me and say, "Now my Aaron will carry on." I had to take over.

In America, too, we found our roles reversed. Allen remained keen, alert, monitoring me constantly and often whispering in a public meeting, "Tell them, Leoda! You tell them" Both he and I learned much patience in those trying days.

During the rehabilitation period, every meal took an hour, because the muscles in his throat were partially paralyzed. He had to concentrate on every swallow of food to be sure it went down. Talking at meal times became a thing of the past. Allen used words only when necessary, so I had to be the conversationalist, the office secretary, the speaker, and his companion. How could we cope?

We played music tapes during meal times. I changed my habits of eating and loitered over my food, so that my husband wouldn't be struggling alone for forty minutes out of every hour at the table. We played Scrabble together, a game we still enjoy.

Our trials were shaping and molding us into becoming more pliable mates. Surely this pleases our Lord. I believe our heavenly Father places great value on longsuffering (which simply means suffering long,) and patience, the result of bearing trials and afflictions with fortitude.

Our situation is far from bleak. Indeed, there are many bright spots, particularly in one of the new skills the Lord has given Allen. He loves people, and small children are always attracted to him. One day we learned of the need for helpers in the church nursery. My husband looked up with interest after reading the plea in the bulletin and asked, "Do you think I could handle this?"

"Of course you could!" I exclaimed. "You'd love it."

So he volunteered for the one-year-olds. He soon found his niche as he lulled crying children to sleep, rocking them lovingly in his rocking chair as would any doting grandpa. His rapport with these little ones has reaped some beautiful benefits. Periodically he receives notes or pictures, one time an Easter card drawn by hand. The senders are three- or four-year-olds who remember their special friend, Mr. Buckwalter, with affection. Their radiant smiles and handshakes with him each Sunday are a constant pay-off for his selfless gift of helps.

God-given gifts are primarily for this purpose—to encourage and build up those around us. It's also a chance to forget ourselves in meeting others' needs. Since each of us automatically exerts an influence, we are responsible before God for the use of the gifts he bestows. I see Allen's love for small children as being very Christ-like; his cooking frees me to write; and I trust that my readership is truly edified by what I have written.

One other gift from the Lord surfaced throughout the years of ministering in India, that of teaching the Scriptures. Several times Child Evangelism Fellowship approached me, asking me to take on childrens' work in Bihar. But each time the Lord held me back, showing me that he wanted me to teach adults. That seemed a formidable task, but the one who calls gives the enabling.

I love to see people with their Bibles open, to watch the glow on their faces as some new truth flashes across their consciousness during the study sessions. To measure spiritual growth in their love for the Lord Jesus Christ and his Word makes all the hours of teaching worthwhile. Watching character traits change, with old habits dropping away, to be replaced by the fruits of the Spirit—that's the real pay-off for night sessions of struggling in prayer for each person by name. The apex of blessing comes when such a one becomes a source of spiritual blessing to others. And the chain goes on.

I'm thinking of Edith, an Anglican pastor's wife who attended my Bible study class for women in Bangalore. As a busy mother of five children, she seemed totally immersed in her family duties, but the call of God to be a more active partner with her husband stirred her heart. She responded, and through the years they have formed a wonderful team.

After retiring from active service in India, they went to Australia, but began filling in for weary pastors both at home and abroad. At this writing, according to our information, they are pastoring an English-speaking church in France until the regular pastor returns.

From that same womens' group in Bangalore came Julie, a beautiful Indian woman, married and mother of several children. She responded to God's call as the Word opened her understanding, and today she has an important position with the Evangelical Fellowship of India, reaching and discipling women all over the nation.

Pamela also lives in Bangalore since marriage. Prior to that, she lived with us in Delhi while teaching in an English-speaking school in the area. Pam gave her heart to the Lord by watching our home-life. Our one-on-one Bible study sessions each day paid off.

She was an eager student, loving and following the Lord Jesus Christ. We sponsored her baptism and wedding.

In Bangalore she started a Christian school that grew and grew until every room except the kitchen was used for classes. Finally she had to leave for health reasons. Then Pam turned to writing, art work, and attendant skills. The Lord has gifted her to write for secular newspapers and magazines.

Currently she is traveling with her husband, who is recognized in India for his communications know-how, and they have formed a team. She illustrates books for children. He publishes and distributes them. We're proud of Pam, and her influence for Jesus Christ throughout the great land of India.

Something special in September? It came as a gift from the Lord, designed to impact others for him. God gives to each one freely, but we can take no credit, for we are but stewards of a treasure held in trust. You and I are answerable to the Lord Jesus Christ. We dare not live unto ourselves!

CHAPTER FIVE

THREE STROKES BUT NOT OUT!

A stroke sometimes gives warning, but Allen missed the cue. My husband has suffered three strokes of varying intensity in the last twenty years. All have left their physical marks upon him, but his spirit continues to stay strong and victorious. Therein lies our story.

The first one hit in Bangalore, South India, early in February 1977, when both of us were fully involved with daily office routines and public relations work in the Indian arm of Far East Broadcasting. Allen was Director for FEBA India; I worked under him as the FEBCOM Fellowship secretary. This was a prayer fellowship that had grown to almost eight thousand members within India. I also prepared a weekly piano program aired over FEBC stations in Manila and the Seychelle Islands.

In the midst of all this activity, the first stroke struck. On a Saturday afternoon, during preparations for going out for the evening, Allen suddenly felt an electric shock from head to foot and managed to get to the bed before telling me.

He could talk, but I noticed that his speech was thickening. Was this a stroke? If so, what should I do? Obviously, he required a doctor and I needed stamina. My mind leaped to Zac and Annie Poonen, a fine Indian couple who lived nearby. I'd write them a note, and hope they were home. Until one or both could come, I'd drink a good, hot cup of tea!

So the cook took the note I scribbled while I drank tea and kept Allen talking to learn the intensity of this new problem. Doctor

Annie soon arrived with her bag while her preacher husband kept the children. She said he figured we needed his wife's medical skills—and he could pray at home as well as here. Zac was right.

Annie checked my husband's symptoms, confirmed my suspicions, and said we must get him to a hospital immediately. On Saturday afternoon? Would there be a doctor available at the mission hospital? Could we get the hospital ambulance?

The Bangalore Baptist Hospital, a wonderful facility which we helped to pray into being, and which now catered to the needs of the Indian and missionary community, had been built on the north side of the city, at least ten miles distant from us. But a dear friend worked there. Clarence would know whom to call.

Usually phones don't work well in India, but that day I got in touch with Clarence Marlam in record time. He somehow contacted a missionary doctor just ready to leave for an afternoon picnic. The doctor sent the family on, ordered the hospital ambulance to pick up his patient, and was there to meet us when we arrived. Within two hours of the stroke's first thrust, Allen was now in a private hospital room, under superb medical attention. I marveled and felt that people must be praying for us.

In Bangalore, a center for Christian activity, news travels fast. Clarence Marlam, a man who seemed to know all the right people, alerted the faithful to prayer. Later, we also learned that our names were featured for that particular day in the *Prayer Challenge*. This meant that all over the United States and Canada, prayer partners were remembering us and our immediate needs. Is it any wonder, then, that the missionary doctors at the Baptist Hospital marveled at the small amount of damage recorded during those first crucial seventy-two hours? Both they and we believed that the Lord halted the stroke exactly when he saw it was enough to accomplish his purposes.

What could be the Lord's purposes? We were midway through our four-year term of FEBA's recovery after a very stormy three years of great stress. International headquarters had tried to Indianize the work, to appoint Indian directors, but the transitional period taxed every ounce of patience and grace that the Indian staff possessed. Three directors came and went in that number of years! So my husband had been called back from Delhi to stabilize everything.

When we moved south to Bangalore, we found a fragmented group of people who needed a lot of loving. The Lord did a miracle of grace among us, and the work was now growing and prospering. New faces and new commitments added zest to those who had become weary of struggle. Now this director, Allen Buckwalter, whom they loved and called "Moses," had been stricken and hospitalized! The staff of more than thirty people banded together to keep FEBA India on an even keel until Allen could return, and they did a splendid job!

I became the "go-between." Johnny, our efficient office manager and Allen's right-hand-man, assumed double duties in administration. Before noon each day I could expect his packet for me to take and read to the boss. But since I couldn't drive, this presented a problem.

Not for long, since Festus, our Indian engineer who had served several years on Operation Mobilization's ship, *Logos*, knew how to handle Allen's BSA motorcycle. He became my driver, taking me to work each morning and later to the hospital before noon. Leaving me there, he would again return for me in the evening and see me home. I was always in Indian garb, so I rode side-saddle on the cycle as do the myriads of young women in the cities where office workers depend on motorized transport.

Anticipation of our daily visits spurred my husband on to exercise his paralyzed right hand and arm, and Festus's daily reports did much to keep staff morale high. During Allen's twenty-one days in the hospital, almost all the staff members managed to pay him a personal visit. We felt that in itself showed the inner healing that God's Spirit had performed in the ranks of FEBA India.

Another beautiful bonding surfaced during those stress-filled days. Committed Christians united throughout Bangalore and Delhi to pray for my husband's recovery, and for FEBA's current needs. One of these was a Malayalee business man nicknamed "Pickle Abraham" to distinguish him from the many other Abrahams in our city. He and his wife owned and operated a factory that produced curry powders, chutneys, and other delicious Indian savories. She was the manager.

Mr. Abraham's wife, Chinnakutty, and I had met about a year before. She requested me to aid in her many Bible study groups in Bangalore. I complied as often as my work permitted, and we soon became dear friends. One day, when I mentioned FEBA India's need for prayer partners, her husband responded curtly, "I have my commitments!" The message came through loud and clear, and though accompanying Chinnakutty for many months, not once did I mention the radio ministry again. However, silence on my part merely meant my talking to the Lord about the matter.

Allen's stroke occurred in February. Money was tight, and we seldom knew from one month to the next whether there would be enough in the bank to pay staff salaries. True, our prayer partners often sent in donations, but we couldn't foresee how, when, or in what quantity our God would supply. It kept us on our faces before him, and this built faith in the staff as they saw visible answers.

Now the end of February was approaching. With Allen in the hospital, the accountant sent an urgent plea for direction since we were short of funds. How could he pay staff? My husband listened quietly, then said, "Tell him to check both accounts—both foreign and domestic, Leoda. The Lord is always faithful." When K. C. Mammen checked the overseas balance, he found that the need had been met! Staff received their allowances on time, and we rejoiced.

That evening, on the last day of February, I was to go with Chinnakutty to one of her prayer groups. A telephone call from Mr. Abraham puzzled me. "Mrs. Buckwalter," he said, "we would like you to come early for tea. Would that be suitable?"

"Why, yes, Mr. Abraham, I think I can manage it."

"Very good, madam," he said in his clipped English. "My driver will come for you half an hour early."

Tea with the Abrahams? Was it somebody's birthday? Perhaps there would be many guests. My thoughts whirled, but when I arrived I discovered this was much more than a mere friendly gesture. My host came directly to the point by asking, "Mrs. Buckwalter, FEBA needs money?"

"Why, yes, Mr. Abraham, FEBA always needs money, but we had enough today to pay salaries. God is so good!" I exclaimed with a smile.

"Yes, yes, God is good—but FEBA needs money! This very day in our morning devotions God told me and my wife that FEBA needs money, so here is our donation." He handed me a sealed envelope.

How could I be polite and resist opening it in their presence? I couldn't! Husband and wife chuckled as I peeked and saw two crisp one thousand rupee notes, This was the largest single donation from any Indian up to that time. It was as though they had given us two thousand dollars!

That began a partnership in missionary radio that has grown through twenty years. The Abrahams quietly sponsored Malayalam programs over the air. Even after her husband's death, Chinnakutty not only continued her commitment, but enlarged her giving to include other languages. When did it begin? When Allen was in the hospital, struggling to regain the use of his right arm and hand.

Ten years passed. Recovery was almost total, except for one permanent disability. He doesn't "think" with the fingers of his right hand. This results in interesting consequences, as when he struggles to button his shirt, or to be sure he has his keys in his hand when he takes them from his pocket. Neither can my husband detect hot or cold with the affected part, so he carefully checks water with his left hand instead of the right one. But when taking injections he gladly proffers his right one, so that he can't feel it. Allen is smart!

Healing and wholeness surely come from the Lord. It may be through medical skills or in direct answer to prayer. I pondered, therefore, the Lord's plan for leaving this one vestige of the first stroke. Could it be something like a sign of singular blessing which we would recognize at a later date? Or is it that our finite minds tend to forget God's goodness unless something be given to us by which to remember? We so soon seem to lose the sense of awe and wonder that accompanied the healing; we take it for granted. I lean toward the second answer, but grant the validity of both.

In September 1986, we celebrated our fiftieth wedding anniversary by an intimate family gathering at our daughter's home. Then we traveled overseas for three months, touching eight different countries and visiting fifteen FEBC installations. Allen took pictures everywhere. With an accumulation of updates from around the world, plus a deeper understanding of what God is accomplishing even in closed countries, we returned home. But first we checked in at FEBC headquarters, then spent an enjoyable Christmas with families in California.

In Seoul, Korea, before we returned to the States, my husband suffered dizziness one day. At the time, Allen and I thought nothing of it except to conclude it came from weariness. Later we recognized it for what it must have been—a warning signal for an impending stroke.

It struck in February 1987. Again, it came silently, as had the first one in Bangalore, India. After eating a normal breakfast, my husband slipped into the living room to his favorite chair in the corner. I didn't notice, but when he called and I heard him speak, both of us realized this was serious. Our family doctor and our daughter came, and an ambulance soon took my husband to Lancaster General Hospital where he stayed for a full month.

This second stroke primarily affected his swallowing and speech. As previously mentioned, it caused major changes in our lifestyle, and required his being fed by a tube through his nose into his stomach for six weeks. Certainly it must have been a harrowing and harassing experience. However, none of us ever heard Allen complain.

Much prayer arose from our church fellowship, and someone took me to the hospital each afternoon where I stayed until our daughter, Joanne, could take me home after work. When Allen was allowed to return home, all of us rejoiced.

Rehabilitation began under the supervision of our dedicated family doctor and a Christian nurse who gave her skills freely to teaching Allen how to swallow again, but he had to do his part! It demanded vigilance and patience, both of which were sometimes stretched to the limit. Now every victory turned into a celebration.

One morning, while my husband labored over his breakfast and I had gone to my typewriter to begin the day's work, we experienced a giant leap forward. He was able to eat pureed food, but taking water presented an insurmountable difficulty, yet his body needed the liquid. We hadn't yet learned of new food products that now thicken liquids safely.

I was busy typing when the Lord's directive came to me clearly, saying, "Leoda, speak to the involuntary muscles in Allen's

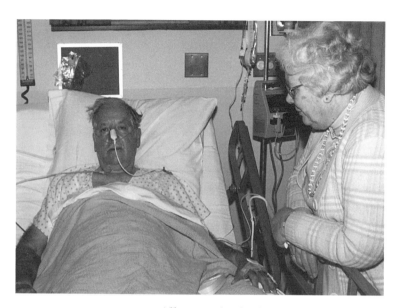

Allen was in the hospital for six weeks.

throat." Involuntary muscles? I didn't even know they existed, but this called for immediate action. I stopped typing and said aloud, "You involuntary muscles in Allen Buckwalter's throat, in the name of Jesus I command you to work in harmony with the others."

It sounded crazy, I admit, but within a couple of minutes my husband came to the bottom of the stairs and called up to the office, "Leoda! I just drank my first glass of water!" He has been speaking to his throat muscles ever since, and God gets the glory.

We all know that learning new habits is not an easy task. Many hours of patient effort builds character. Is that the Lord's purpose in sending trials? I know that many days we despaired of progress. In fact, I played a little game with Allen to help him speak clearly. Whenever his speech slurred I would say, "Pardon?" and he would repeat it clearly, thinking that I was really getting hard of hearing. I didn't tell him any differently, and one day he said in disgust, "You really are getting hard of hearing! We must get you a hearing aid." But today Allen's speech doesn't often betray the long struggle, nor his perseverance to attain this degree of capability. And we celebrate this victory!

No, that's not the end of the story, for three months after the second stroke, the third struck, hitting his right leg primarily and his right side secondarily. Already affected members, such as his right hand, suffered a setback, and when he tried to walk he listed like a ship at sea in a storm. Our family doctor brought him a walker. Later I went to town and bought a cane. But very soon my husband discarded both. He has an iron will, and he serves a living God!

It is but human for our undisciplined minds to scream, "Why, God? Why do you allow this to happen to us?" We tend to run away from suffering like little children. But I recall an incident years before that bears upon this very question.

Allen and I were attending an annual convention of the Evangelical Fellowship of India. It was in Calcutta, with the meetings held under a large canvas tent set on the compound of a church. Corrie Ten Boom was one of the main speakers, and as usual, I served as pianist. But this time both the speakers and piano were on the same platform.

So I sat behind Corrie Ten Boom on the platform as she gave her message in English with her quaint, attractive Dutch brogue. To illustrate her point, she took a piece of embroidery from her little case that always accompanied her, and opened it with the wrong side facing the audience. She held it high for all to see—a mass of colored threads, knots, lacking design and purpose. All the while she spoke of trials and troubles that assail us as Christians.

I could see the back side of the embroidery. It was a strikingly beautiful piece of art forming a picture of a cross under a crown. "That's what God is doing," Corrie repeatedly emphasized. "He sees what you and I don't see, because he has the master plan." She then showed the audience the right side.

So I found my heart comforted when trials seemed to overwhelm us. Our Lord had not forsaken us; he knew what he was doing, and we could safely trust him. Was it any wonder, then, that two major blessings resulted from Allen's strokes in 1987?

The first signal of divine approbation brought immediate hope for the days ahead; the second changed the course of our ministry and thereby had far-reaching effects. Let's look at them, since through his workings we learn more about God.

The first was the release of *Out of the Cobra's Clutches*, a book Allen wrote prior to our retirement, during his last year in FEBA Delhi. This was the conversion story of Ratnam, a Brahman priest who worshiped the cobra. Taking place around the turn of the century, the account had been preserved, written and verified by Ratnam's great granddaughter, our friend, Mrs. Margaret Edwards. She wanted the story published, so Allen spent many hours working on it.

As happens to many a good project, it lay idle until we settled in Elizabethtown. One day the manuscript again came to light and my husband began rewriting. When it was finally ready for publication, Evangel Publishing House accepted it, their artist drew intriguing illustrations, and the book was released at about the same time as Allen's third stroke!

Three strikes and out? Not in God's economy, for he isn't finished with us yet. Can I adequately share the sense of exhilaration when such a work is not only accomplished, but begins a journey of blessing others through its pages? *Out of the Cobra's Clutches* became a favorite with many readers. It is now out of print, but it played a big part in helping us to hope for a continued outreach, regardless of the author's physical disabilities.

God's second blessing resulted from the pruning we went through in those days. Jesus talked about it with his disciples just before he went to the cross. The evening before, he said, "I am the true vine, and My Father is the vinedresser. Every branch in Me that does not bear fruit He takes away; and every branch that bears fruit He prunes, that it may bear more fruit.... I am the vine, you are the branches. He who abides in Me, and I in him, bears much fruit; for without Me you can do nothing. If anyone does not abide in Me, he is cast out as a branch and is withered; and they gather them and throw them into the fire, and they are burned. If you abide in Me, and My words abide in you, you shall ask what you desire, and it shall be done for you. By this My Father is glorified, that you bear much fruit; so you will be My disciples" (John 15:1, 2 and 5-8, NKJV).

So the pruning took place in our lives, and much of the former activities ceased. The Lord replaced extensive touring from one mission conference to another with our meeting intimate prayer groups on a monthly basis. Allen enjoys driving, and the lasting friendships formed through these regular contacts with the Lord's people made every trip worthwhile.

Moreover, God hears and answers prayer, so the results of those years are visible. Four missionary units (two married couples and two ladies) are on the mission field today engaged in missionary radio. All but one came from Pennsylvania! The other came from India as a student to study in the States. We met her in Delhi when she was yet a Buddhist. Now she is actively engaged in bringing the gospel to her own people and we praise God.

When did the prayer meetings begin? When Allen's strokes took him off the platform and placed him in the pew. Three strokes, but not out! We're still in the fray for our Lord Jesus Christ, and we rejoice in the victories which we have personally seen in ourselves and others. Each of us impacts other people either for good or otherwise. They in turn touch those whom God brings to them, so the chain continues. We have a sacred responsibility to be true to our Lord in all matters, and to trust and obey even when we do not understand.

In conclusion, I want to share the testimony of an Ethiopian lady who heard the gospel through a friend of ours, Esther Russell. Esther and Murray spent twenty-three years in Africa, and returned to the States in 1982. Since here they have been in active retirement. For them this meant pastoring in Presbyterian churches, and later working with prisoners.

In a recent letter, Esther wrote, "Aster Dibaba is a beautiful 'daughter' who has been in the States for about thirteen years. She is a vibrant and growing woman of faith. A few months ago she sat in our living room and told me something that puts things in perspective.

"She is a paraplegic who only manages to walk with artificial legs. She said, 'You know, Mama Aster (we share the same name,) I should be a beggar sitting along the road in an Ethiopian village. I am a cripple, and a woman! But you told me about Jesus and that I am precious to him and how he loved me.' She continued, telling of the many miracles that have brought her to the place where she is now—a very successful teacher in Seattle, a recording artist, a mother of two, also the wife of a fine Ethiopian pastor, a counselor, etc.

"She continued, 'I have been in America for many years now. There are many churches, and radio ministries, but there is something I have never found here. Do you remember how young people would be willing to walk for hours through any weather, on nearly empty stomachs and many of them unwell, just to have the privilege of coming to a Christian school? Do you remember how, when we would have a spiritual life conference in Dembi Dollo, people would travel for days to attend? I have never seen that hunger, that passionate search for God here."

That is quite an indictment against the complacency of the American religious scene! Who here is willing to suffer for the Lord's sake, rather than seeking our own good?

Esther Russell concluded her letter, "*Ornamental Christians* is a term I found lately. Pew sitters, those who go to churches for stimulation or entertainment, burned out pastors—discouraged as they try to meet the demands of the laity, etc. The ever-increasing rush of religious activity and competition today, generally speaking, makes us miss the meaningful gatherings under a tree when we sang to the beat of a native drum. There the gospel was clearly spoken with simplicity."

How true! My heart echoes "Amen" when I think back to all the precious moments spent in discipling new Christians. Having renounced Satan worship and animism, they turned to the Lord Jesus who was so very real to them. They loved him and worshiped him with every fiber of their being; they gladly withstood persecution for his sake. As a result, the seedling church took root, grew, and flourished.

Will that happen here? Yes, when we see the same type of courage and commitment in the face of opposition! Yes, when the Spirit of God can show "Jesus" to a watching world each day, regardless of (or perhaps in the midst of) trials and testings.

Where does the beautiful lotus flower grow? In the mud! It flourishes in marshy places, proclaiming beauty and grace. That's what the Lord desires to do in and through each one of his children. Let's give him a chance, knowing that someone just might glimpse God's transcending glory!

CHAPTER SIX

THERE'S SOMETHING ABOUT A BOOK!

When people walk into our home, they soon discover our obvious love for books. Books are in every room of the house except the bedroom. You can find bookshelves in the guest room upstairs and in Allen's office. Step into our good-sized eat-in kitchen and you see an ingenious piece of furniture designed and built by my husband. We affectionately call it "the whatzit," since it holds his prized tape recorder/radio, a speaker, a rack for tapes, and shelves and drawers that hold miscellaneous items such as tapes, supplies (meaning wires, screws, and such mysterious things!) But there's still ample room on those shelves for albums and plenty of books.

Both of us love good books. Westerns and romances caught my fancy during my teenage years, and Zane Grey, Grace Livingstone Hill, and Louisa Alcott became my favorite authors. But I also enjoyed Shakespeare. The study of English literature broadened my perceptions, opening new worlds to my eager spirit.

True, this love for reading came before the invention of television. Also, we were nurtured as young people by our wonderful high school and college professors who imparted the joy and value of such old-fashioned habits as reading. This took place for Allen and me in a small but effective Christian high school and junior college founded in Upland, California, by my maternal grandfather, Bishop C.C. Burkholder, in 1920.

I remember Grandpa as a man of commanding physique, with a rare merging of qualities that won the confidence of each community where he resided. A pioneer who proved he could accept new thoughts and ideas, he became a self-taught man, albeit his not having more than a grammar school education.

Though reared in a conservative Mennonite community in Pennsylvania, Christian Burkholder was interested in scientific inventions and believed in broadening educational privileges for all. I remember him saying often with twinkling eyes, "My, My! Isn't it just now wonderful how the Lord works!"

Is it incredible, then, that Grandpa bought one of the first three cars in his town? He couldn't drive, nor did he learn, but he encouraged his sons to drive, and thoroughly enjoyed riding in the Reo. Moreover, he bought a radio as soon as they became available. His encouragement to the next generation to follow their dreams marked him as a true leader.

Grandpa lived what he preached. His pioneer spirit led him from Pennsylvania to Kansas where he was soundly converted and later ordained as a minister. He also found his wife in Kansas, a daughter of Bishop and Mrs. Samuel Zook of Abilene. As a carpenter, Grandpa earned a living for his growing family of six children, one of whom died in infancy. My mother, Katie Florence Burkholder, was the second eldest.

For nine years Chris and Fannie Burkholder helped in the church work on a voluntary basis, but being a pioneer at heart, he couldn't stay any longer in Kansas. The call of the West moved Grandpa first to Arizona, then in 1901 to Upland, California, then known as North Ontario. With his skill as a contractor, he built many houses in the fast growing area at the foot of the San Antonio mountains. The highest peak was known as "Old Baldy" to local settlers.

My grandparents worked hard to establish a Brethren in Christ Church among the new settlers, and here they resided until they died. It was in Upland, at the foot of "Old Baldy," that my brother Joe and I joined Grandpa and Grandma as members of their immediate family. We came as waifs from India, and lived with them for the next ten or more years.

I loved my grandfather's inner strength and gentle ways. He had distinct likes and dislikes, but never forced them on others. Instead, he let the Lord do the molding. Because he faithfully modeled the messages that he preached, we believed what grandpa said. Knowing his own limitations and also the power of a risen Lord in his own life, this great man reached out beyond himself to give the next generation, including us, a chance to follow our dreams. Through his vision, and largely by his effort and encouragement, Beulah College opened its doors in Upland in 1920. My grandfather was elected the first president, a post he carried until his death in 1931.

He left this world on a Friday night, with immediate family gathered around his bed, and a houseful of people who waited quietly for what they knew would be a triumphant end to a well-lived life. They were right, for that evening I witnessed the joy of Grandpa's passing from one "room" to another! I stood at the end of the bed, and saw the peace on his face. I heard him say, "I hear the bells ringing." He looked toward the window as though listening, and Aunt Adeline said softly, "The angels have come for him." We didn't see them, but she was right. We were standing on holy ground.

How did Mother, Joe, and I happen to be there? Seven years before, my father, Henry Light Smith, went to be with the Lord while I was in boarding school in Darjeeling, India. He died of confluent smallpox, a disease so dread that Mother sent my brother, aged five, to missionaries in Supaul while she cared for Daddy with the help of his dear friend, Amos Dick. The end came quickly, and Daddy's grave in Saharsa, India, bears mute evidence to his giving his life for the sake of the gospel.

Mother was also stricken with smallpox, but the Lord raised her up again. We stayed in India for two more years until Amos and Nellie Dick's return to North America for home leave. They brought my brother Joe and me to New York City where mother's youngest sister, Viola, met us. For three months she lived with us in the home of our great aunt and uncle, the Stauffers, in Millersville, Pennsylvania. That summer my grandparents came from California to the East coast, and took us to our new home.

I was eleven and my brother seven when all this happened. America seemed very strange to us. We were somehow "different" in our manner of speech, dress, thought patterns, and habits. No wonder we found it difficult to adjust to a completely new lifestyle! But God brought us into a loving Christian family that helped mold and nurture us through this transitional period. And Mother joined us three years later.

During those early days, my brother and I discovered the Upland Public Library, just one block from our house. It presented the chance to slip away and hide with a good book, and no doubt this helped stabilize us when we needed to just be ourselves!

Grandpa used to monitor all my reading, making sure it met his high standards. Only once or twice do I recall his taking a book back to the library because it had something in it he didn't consider worthy. Interestingly, I must have inherited some of his love for pioneer stories. He certainly did not restrict my reading them.

After coming to Upland, I finished grammar school, high school, and college before marrying Allen Buckwalter in September 1936. We served in a country pastorate north of Morrison, Illinois, for several years, then sailed for India in the fall of 1939. Upon returning to my former homeland as a missionary I learned I had fallen heir to my father's beautiful library. It was like finding gold! His wealth of good, hard-cover classics included literature, art, and many miscellaneous works of high literary merit.

I still use my personal copy of *A Dictionary of the Hindee Language*, written by "J.D. Bate, missionary." This second edition of this masterful work has been considered a classic ever since it was printed at the Indian Press in Allahabad in 1918. It is a treasure that I found in my parents' library.

In that same collection was an English copy of the Koran. During our first term in North Bihar, before leaving on an evangelistic tour one winter season, I removed that book from the bookcase and took it along. While in camp, malaria laid me low. During my week of recuperation, I read everything I could find in those Islamic scriptures concerning Jesus of Nazareth, the prophet. In a matter of days, that updated knowledge proved to be the bridge that opened the door of an entire Moslem community to our gospel teams. To people who had never before heard of the love of God for them in Jesus Christ, we had the freedom to go where we willed in their community, and were treated with the utmost hospitality. It was an amazing experience! Where could I find an English copy of the Koran? In my father's library.

In 1960 we moved eight hundred miles from North Bihar to India's capital city, New Delhi. Not having any U-Haul trailers or moving vans, nor even interstate highways as we do here in America, we had to limit our luggage to whatever could be sent by train. We were pioneering, much as Grandpa Burkholder did, answering a call to enter a new ministry—missionary radio. We didn't know yet where we would live, so it seemed wise to place the greater part of our possessions in storage at one of the mission stations, and await developments. Daddy's library and many of our household items went into that category. However, we did take some prized volumes, such as the Hindi dictionary, with us. They became doubly precious in light of what transpired.

As happens so often in tropical countries, termites got into those boxes and riddled everything edible. We lost many pictures and all of the books! A sad ending to our tale, for sure, but such losses are part of the price we pay for living overseas.

Now we are back in the States, living in this land of plenty. Reentry pains or culture shock in reverse again hit. I have already described some of those feelings and insecurities that beset me, especially during the initial years of resettlement. Even yet I feel a twinge of conscience when I throw away plastic containers or "junk mail." Waste here seems so prevalent, and the value of used articles so low in comparison to India, where anything reusable is valuable.

I wondered whether I was alone in this, so thought it best to tap into a personal source of information. Accordingly, I have contacted almost a hundred people whom we knew in India, who are now living in the States. This roster contains students, retired missionaries, several Indian graduate students, and at least one Indian who now heads up a world-wide organization. Their replies vary, naturally, depending on their past, how many years they lived in India, how many years they have been here, and to what degree they have become one with the present American scene. I'd like to share some of these replies. Unless otherwise noted, names have been changed to protect their identity.

First of all, we have testimonials from three who came in their student years and remained. The first we will call Twila, the second will be Clive, and the third will come under her own name, Colleen.

With her husband and four children, Twila lives in one of the southern states and is active in church work. She came from a missionary family, attended Woodstock in the lower Himalayas until graduating from high school, then returned to the States to live with an uncle and aunt until her parents came on home leave. Here's her testimony:

"The hardest part was leaving my friends, many of whom I had been in school with since kindergarten. I had a very special relationship with almost all of my graduating class. When you have shared so much of your life with people like that, you can't help but bond in a very special way.

"We lived in dorms together, went to school and church together, and spent all our spare time together. I remember moonlight hikes, overnight camping, sports activities, school concerts and plays, devotionals, and retreats. We shared every aspect of our growing years, even more than brothers and sisters would. I felt like my heart was torn in two the day when I had to say 'goodbye.' I knew I would never see many of my dear friends again.

"The missionaries who worked with the same mission as we did had become very close to us. We called them Aunt or Uncle, and they truly were our aunts and uncles. I feel more connected because of childhood bonding times, I'm sure, than I do to my flesh and blood aunts and uncles.

"I went through a very definite grieving time. Even now, almost thirty years later, it doesn't take much to get a nostalgic lump in my throat."

It is as though Twila takes a deep breath here, then adds with a smile, "But I was very excited about each new experience ahead of me. I felt like I had just landed on another planet and I wanted to explore it. I remember walking several miles (we walked everywhere in India) to a Murphy's Five and Ten Store. The assortment of merchandise and all the bright colors were both beautiful and overwhelming."

Now she pauses, then confesses, "When I first returned to the States, I had some problems with my self image. I felt like I looked different. I knew I talked different, with my very British Indian accent, but I didn't mind that. But I felt that when I walked into a room, I just looked foreign to people. I felt very homely, largely because of my clothes. But a boy cousin near my age helped me more than he'll ever know, because he gave me compliments."

Twila concludes, saying, "The hardest thing for me to get used to in this very wealthy society was the terrible waste. I couldn't believe the food that was thrown away. It seemed a sin to throw away empty jars and coffee cans (that I throw away now) and wrapping paper (we ironed ours and used it over and over, and I still do that.) I could hardly believe all the lights people would have turned on. And to top it all, people would talk like they had so little, and say 'if only I was richer...' To me it seemed they had *so* much!"

Twila speaks not only for herself, but for numerous others who have felt the same way when they came to America. They are hybrids, representing two cultures. A little bit of loving and a lot of understanding will go far to make them feel at home. Have you hugged your "hybrid" today?

Clive has a different temperament, no doubt, and instead of staying in India until he was older, he moved back to the States with his family when he was 15. He has lived here for thirty-four years, and has a good job teaching art and computer in elementary schools.

Clive says, "I found it relatively easy to adjust to American ways. I attribute this to my relatively young age (15) and that we experienced the culture through furloughs. Also, I hadn't really established strong cultural, religious, or political ideals. Perhaps the area of most difficulty was social life in school, establishing new friends. It took a full year to feel assimilated into the group."

I think I can identify most clearly with Clive, in that I, too, came from India at a young age and was nurtured by those who tried desperately to know and understand our problems. To them this became priority, especially since mother was still in India. Grandma and the others loved to talk about India, and they tried to make us feel one of them.

We had an interesting assortment of people living in the Burkholder home at any given time. In between guests, on a regular basis there was first of all, Grandma (always there, and always available.) She took in washing to help meet expenses, and taught me to iron. I didn't realize that I was thus helping to pay for my piano lessons! But, incidentally, she taught me well, and I have enjoyed ironing ever since. Grandpa, as previously mentioned, did a great deal of traveling, but still exerted a strong influence upon us youngsters. My young aunt Viola, whom Joe and I love very dearly, stayed home at nights but worked daily as a nurse in a Los Angeles hospital, some thirty-five miles away. Living nearby was Uncle Alvin and his wife, Aunt Vera. Alvin seemed more like an older brother than an uncle, since he was only five years of age when my mother got married.

I must yet mention another member of the family, Wilson Hoffman, a boarder for thirty years! Wilson was a fixture—winding the grandfather clock, doing certain tasks with punctuality, maintaining his own lifestyle, but always there. So much so that when Grandpa and Grandma died, Uncle Alvin and Aunt Vera built an extra room onto their house so that Wilson would have a home. With the grandfather clock for comfort, Wilson lived on with the Burkholders until he, too, had to leave this life.

Now I've reminisced a long time, while Colleen stands waiting in the wings. I do want you to meet her, for she is very special. She's a true hybrid, born into a missionary family with an American father and an Indian mother. Colleen Townsley Hager, of Garland, Texas, came to the States in 1971 and now serves the Greater Dallas community of churches as Director of Communications.

Colleen notes that there's a lack of good parenting in America, and that churches and denominations have allowed the family structures to break down. Here she is to speak for herself.

"Basically, I treasure my heritage and find myself always identifying as 'from India' and telling of my half U.S. and half Indian roots! I *always* get a very receptive response. I find, however, that the U.S. is deteriorating in quality, values, etc. I support no particular political party, but find our present Washington scene tasteless and corrupt."

Recently, Colleen had the joy of showing her husband and children her homeland. Their Christmas greeting said, "We four will long remember 1996 for the year we trekked to India, my native home. A long-cherished dream became a reality and Gordon, Robert (13), and Jessica (10) were finally able to see the charm and beauty which peppered my childhood and adolescent memories."

Like a golden chain, the family weaves these recollections together, and anyone who has lived in India knows how true they are. I quote only about half of them:

"Saffron sunsets behind the Taj Mahal; pungent spices; delicate temple bells; warm embraces; expressions of love from family; the heat; jasmine strands in Jessica and Colleen's hair; curious stares at Gordon's t-shirts; connections with Colleen's past in South Indian villages..."

Anyone who has lived in such a land for many years finds life in the West like Twila did when she said, "I felt like I had landed on another planet." When two worlds vary so vastly, comparison seems useless. We just try to "turn the page" and begin over again. And I wondered whether others felt the same way. Here's a sampling from missionary friends who retired in the States or Canada after spending years in India or some other foreign land.

One of our friends from the African Inland Mission now lives in a missionary retirement home in Florida. She writes that she could hardly get used to ladies wearing slacks to church. Also, she finds it difficult to build strong friendships outside the missionary community, and concedes it might be because missionaries understand missionaries!

After being used to cooking everything "from scratch," the convenience of TV dinners and other prepared foods seemed very strange, but she adds with candor, "However, I'm finding this easy to do." Our friend had to become used to telephoning instead of paying a personal visit, but she adds, "I like this."

Another friend who lives in a missionary home elsewhere in the southland says she found one of her biggest adjustments was to the South. Having served many years in North India, this would undoubtedly be true. Both she and her husband are active in retirement, doing volunteer visitation and participating in classes held by the church they attend. She says candidly that she would like to forget the whole political scene in the U.S., but since her husband served in World War II and is therefore much interested in what is happening in the nation, she can't just turn away and ignore it. They have been in the States for a little over ten years.

And then there is Beth Brunemeier who used to work in India and Nepal. When we were in India, we visited her in a hospital north of Kathmandu, only four miles away from the city, but it seemed to us that we had stepped way back in time! Beth left Nepal at the close of 1987 because she had a torn retina and couldn't return.

Where does she live now? In Las Vegas, Nevada, with a sister who worked there for twenty years. Understandably, then, Beth finds driving in Las Vegas traffic "horrendous!" Let's get the story direct from Beth Brunemeier.

"This once dusty desert crossroads now has over one million here. The December 1996 *National Geographic* explains it! Fifty thousand Asians live here, mostly international university students and many of them Afghans and their friends, etc. They present a huge open door of seekers. Only age (mid-seventies,) weakness in my spine, and lack of time and energy hold me back.

"Our church is 'inner city,' and is the largest in Nevada. We have every imaginable race and need in our 'integrated' membership, but almost nobody is still with their first spouse!..."

Now Beth seems to take a deep breath before adding, "We see demonic infiltration going on here in the U.S. generally, in moral freefall. 'Just as it was in the days of Noah!' And my heart says 'Come quickly, Lord Jesus! Help us to get the lost into the ark now and not dissipate our strength looking back."

It is a fitting challenge, Beth, and we thank you for sharing the burden of your heart.

Beth also leads into what I yet want to say. We have talked about literature, art, beautiful scenery, and much else in this chapter full of memories and adjustments to a new land. But the last testimonial has pointed the way out of a sense of personal loss and grief over the past.

Both Beth and I, and a host of others who have survived trauma and heartache, have done so because the Word of God and the Spirit of God were present in our lives. Books may come and books may go, but the Word of the Lord stands forever. That Word is the Bible!

It was in India, when I was a missionary, that the Bible truly became my fortress and my strength. I had known much about it, for I had studied many books about the Book; now as a missionary in India I learned to study its pages, to stand upon its revelation of

Jesus Christ as my only hope. It was in India I had the joy of teaching forty key verses of Scripture to the new believers who had just stepped out of animism and Satan worship into the matchless love of God.

Those new believers lacked commentaries and all the helpful literature found in abundance at any good Christian book store in America, but they had the Word of God in their hearts and that sustained them through all kinds of persecution. Truly the Bible is a fortress! We can run to it, and be safe when we trust in its amazing revelation of our living, risen Lord Jesus Christ.

I titled this chapter, "There's something about a book," but now let's go one step further and proclaim that there's something about The Book which makes it different from all others. How? Read on for the rest of the story.

CHAPTER SEVEN

MORE THAN A NODDING ACQUAINTANCE

My cousin Kathryn and I discovered each other on our first visit to California. I was five and she was four. We soon began to consider ourselves as "twin sisters," and wanted to dress alike. We commonly shared one Grandpa, and I quickly adopted her other one, calling him "Grandpa Byer."

It is to Grandpa Byer that today I owe special thanks for motivating us young people to memorize Scripture. He offered the youth rewards, promising one penny per verse. As an eleven-year-old, I immediately went after the Psalms and short passages that appealed to me. Those Scriptures became part of me, since Grandpa Byer maintained strict rules, expecting careful, methodical work. Today, those verses stand firmly entrenched in my memory. I don't remember how much money I thus earned, but the pennies were much less than the "gold" I received! The Book began to become real to me.

During my college years, all of us young people studied many books about the Book. I did especially, since I minored in Religion, with my major in Philosophy. However, much that I learned remained theory until tested in the pressures of missionary life when we returned to the land of my birth. In fact, during my first term my assignment included teaching children Bible during the week and an adult Sunday school class each Sunday morning. This presented a tremendous challenge to simplify great theological concepts learned in Pasadena College, and now use them for nurturing biblically illiterate students! I had studied under Dr. H. Orton Wiley, who tested his material on us theology students while writing his own systematic theology masterpiece!

Need I confess I fell far short? But I learned to use and make my own flannelgraph materials for teaching doctrinal truth. Flannelgraph was a new and viable medium in those days. Much of the time we didn't have resources other than the Bible. Therefore, in order to prepare ourselves more thoroughly, on our first home leave we entered the Biblical Seminary in New York City, and signed up for a concentrated summer course.

Because our studies were so intense, the seminary made us students eat out to ensure our getting the exercise we needed. Little matter, for those classes revitalized my life! I learned to study the Book. The Bible came alive because our professors taught us not only content, but method. They gave us a skill that we can use anywhere, and at any time.

My husband and I drank it all in, with the Spirit of God reviving our thirsty hearts. Neither of us realized it then, but summer school (tucked in between deputation meetings) was the Lord's gracious provision to equip us for the assignment we faced on our return to India.

While yet in America, we were appointed to the adjoining district in North Bihar to open a mission station among the Santals. These tribals had settled centuries before in the hills south of India's sacred river, Ganges. With thousands of Santals migrating northward to clear jungles and become share croppers for wealthy Hindu landlords, they now presented a wide open opportunity for hearing and responding to the gospel of Jesus Christ.

To aid us, the Lord sent Benjamin Mirandy, a converted witch doctor. He, too, came from Santal Parganas, the "mother country" across the Ganges. His zeal, along with his knowledge of customs and religious background of the Santals, proved invaluable. But Allen and I soon realized that we, too, must use Santali to truly be effective. Why? This tribal people, though surrounded by non-Santals, yet managed to preserve their own identity. They loved their mother tongue.

Our appeal for time off for language study resulted in a two-month leave, during which time we lived with an American missionary couple on a large compound in the heart of Santal Parganas. Time was short, so we soaked in as much as possible concerning Santal customs and background. And then, having gotten only the basics of Santali, an intricate language that does not resemble in any way the Hindi we had studied, we had to return to our work in North Bihar.

To nurture the new believers who were increasing, I spent hours helping them memorize Scriptures in Santali to provide something solid on which to stand when faced with persecution in their villages. I began to learn that a person doesn't merely teach "lessons"; a true teacher teaches each person, starting, if possible, where the individual lives. The task of the teacher is to make biblical truth relevant and so plain that those truths become foundational in everyday walk and witness.

To these new believers in North Bihar, persecution came early. Often it meant death threats! They indeed needed to know that Jesus loves them, that he conquered Satan on the cross, and that the ultimate victory in this unfolding battle of the ages is his alone. When we trust the Lord Jesus, we are trusting the Conqueror!

The Santals understood, since they live very close to the spirit world. Visions and dreams and demonic activity are common among them, but peace and joy come only after they believe on Jesus Christ. Theirs is a religion of fear, trying to appease the evil spirits whom they call *bongas*. The great master, Satan, is known to them by the place where he is supposed to live. They call him *Marang Buru* (literally, the great mountain). Why don't the Santals call him by his rightful name? They know it, but they fear to even whisper it!

I remember the tremendous hush that would fall on any audience when any of us Christians would be telling of Christ being the victor over Satan. It was as though they feared even to breathe! What would happen to them and their loved ones? Surely we jeopardized the delicate balance they sought to maintain in the village by our enthusiastic projection of Jesus Christ as Lord. How would they know it was true?

They tested him out through prayer, and were amazed at the dreams, visions, and miracles of healing which resulted. New believers were overjoyed at these manifestations, and became more bold in their witness. In turn, more and more seekers sought to know whether this Jesus story was true. They wanted to read it for themselves!

This led to classes in adult literacy, so that each one could read the Word of God personally. And that led to more believers, more baptisms, and finally to Bible institutes which we missionaries held as a sacred trust from God.

My first student was a Santal teenager named Paul Hembrom. Allen and I were still in Barjora when Paul, aged sixteen, was sent to our orphanage school. He soon asked for individual Bible study, and I started meeting with him each week. But often he would say, "Memsahib, could we meet tomorrow? I'm not quite ready."

Then I learned that Paul wasn't merely studying his lesson; he was memorizing the entire portion of Scripture! This zealous boy held tremendous potential for becoming a mighty man of God, but the Lord soon called him home to glory. He died of tuberculosis soon after we left on our first furlough. When we returned from home leave, we were appointed to Banmankhi to open a mission station among the Santals.

Arriving there in March 1951, we found a total of eight Santal Christians in the entire district (about the size of a county in the States). But the Santal church soon took root with each one winning one. They brought neighbors and friends to the Lord; we discipled them. Allen and I, though members of every evangelistic team or thrust, sought to remain in the background. Santals won Santals; missionaries taught them the Scriptures.

About a year or two into this exciting task, we chose seven key people whom we privately called "the prophets." We could foresee these as our future leadership, and time has verified it. When my brother Joe and his wife joined us in Banmankhi as teachers, we began training them seriously. Although having classes for all the Santal believers, we kept "the prophets" in a group by themselves for a period of three years. For these, Joe and I spent long hours breaking the Word into bite sizes so that each one would understand. We wanted the entire class to become men and women of faith.

Why? Because the human heart rejoices in the spectacular! That's what usually makes a testimony. People tend to hang onto miracles, signs and wonders, even though the Word of God explicitly teaches that "the just shall live by *faith*" (Hab. 2:4). Santal leaders must learn to lead the believers in a daily walk of faith. To do that, our "prophets" must learn to trust when they cannot see! As you and I know, that's not easy.

In God's school, all of us must learn the same lesson. Christ was always looking for faith and was often disappointed. The study of faith becomes the focal point for doctrinal teaching in Paul's letters to young churches. And as I mentioned, Jesus Christ, the great Master Teacher, made it a major subject. Indeed, the entire Gospel of John presents an insightful study of belief and unbelief. We do well to take a serious look at faith from Christ's vantage point.

Walking by faith and living in good relationship with both God and man comes through disciplined living in the valleys of life. People don't often live alone in a valley! They are part of a society that may treat them harshly, especially if they stand openly for the Lord Jesus. Living for him brought even death threats to some of our Santals in North Bihar. For Holy Ann, an Irish saint who lived a century earlier in a completely different culture, it meant serving as a young girl under a cruel master and mistress.

As the story goes, Holy Ann struggled day after day to carry water up a steep hill because the well on the premises had run dry. One evening, exhausted, she laid her cause before the Lord, asking him to once more fill the well with fresh, beautiful water. Then, content with the outcome, she went to sleep.

Upon rising next morning she gaily took her bucket and went to the well. "Where are you going?" someone asked. She exclaimed, "The Lord has filled the well with water!" The girl told the truth! But her hearers thought her crazy. But it was water, all eighty-five feet of it, and the well never went dry again. That's the way faith works. This girl walked by faith in her "valley." She believed in the midst of fellow unbelievers. They nicknamed her "Holy Ann," but they couldn't deny her relationship with her Lord, nor his care for her when in need. She walked by faith, and had more than a nodding acquaintance with her God.

The Santal believers also learned this lesson. As neighbors and family members noted their consistent Christian walk, the church expanded. That's when leadership took over. Benjamin, Patras,

Stephen and Philip, all members of "the prophets" class, became ordained ministers. Hanok preached for a neighboring mission, but Dina served as a flaming evangelist among her own people. And Daniel still receives due honor for his courageous stand for Christ in those early days. Disowned by his father for taking public baptism as a Christian, Daniel remained in the village throughout a long ordeal which I have written about in *The Chief's Son*. His many years of service as a deacon in the church is also noteworthy.

Training lay leadership continued to be an integral part of the missionary thrust among the Santals in North Bihar. Second-generation Christians have carried the gospel into the neighboring country of Nepal, and established new churches. Now those new believers have a vision for going even farther with the gospel. One wonders where God will set the boundaries when his children readily follow!

We completed an exhilarating and exhausting term of over six years among the Santals and returned to the States on furlough. I felt emotionally drained. Still in the throes of adjustments to America, the Lord's question to me one unforgettable night in Upland, California, touched me to the quick. He asked pointedly, "Leoda, what are you doing here?"

I sighed, and said wearily, "Dear Lord, I'm on furlough." Meaning, of course, that I hoped I wouldn't have to do anything, because vegetating for awhile looked tremendously appealing. It was a very human reaction, and I know the Lord understands our physical limitations, but the conversation didn't end there.

After becoming uneasy with silence, I asked, "Dear Lord, what do you want me to do?"

"I want you to do what you did in India among the Santals. Teach the Word."

Astounded, I began hedging. The battle accelerated as all the hindrances to such a course of action arose in my mind during those night hours. Me teach adults in America? In this sophisticated land? How could I ever do that? Does anyone desire such simple teaching? Are there hungry people here, and if so, where are they? I must be imagining things!

But the Lord made it very clear that he would take all responsibility for details if I would be willing to obey his commands. That birthed the Community Bible Clubs in and around Upland, California, during the next number of months. When we returned to India a little over a year later, my three helpers and I were teaching nineteen clubs a week in a radius of thirty miles. I personally taught eleven a week!

I learned much in those days. We consistently used the Gospel of John and worked only with ladies. Each group began when a neighbor invited others into her home for Bible Study. They varied from perhaps half-a-dozen women to twenty or more. We never asked last names, for even then (in the late 1950s) non-churched women lived mixed-up lives! But heart hungers soon surfaced as the Spirit of God used his Word to touch each individual. We began to see conversions and life transformations. It was thrilling!

When Allen, Joanne, and I returned to India after our extended home leave, the Community Bible Clubs gave us a tremendous send-off, promising to back us in prayer and with finances. They were true to their promise. During our twenty years with the Far East Broadcasting Associates of India, the clubs paid our monthly rent in Delhi and Bangalore. I assure you that the Lord knew what he was doing that night in Upland when he insisted that it wasn't time for me to vegetate!

When is it time? When one retires? Not in our experience, for three years into our "retirement" I again heard that same question, "Leoda, what are you doing here?" That was in 1984.

The inquiry sounded very familiar, and I confess that in weariness and pain I answered, "Lord, please let me first become adjusted to America. That was California. Remember? This is Pennsylvania. Already I see cultural differences. I don't know these thought patterns and habits. How can I ever teach?"

But the Lord said, "You can learn. All I want is your will."

So it came again—that call to total obedience, regardless of personal cost. It seems to me to be the Lord's theme song, for he keeps saying, as he did to the disciples, "Most assuredly, I say to you, unless a grain of wheat falls into the ground and dies, it remains alone; but if it dies, it produces much grain. He who loves his life will lose it, and he who hates his life in this world will keep it for eternal life. If anyone serves Me, let him follow Me: and where I am, there My servant will be also. If any one serves Me, him My Father will honor" (John 12:24-26, NKJV).

Was my Lord waiting patiently for three years for me to "settle in" and accept the new soil in which he had planted me? I verily believe it, and I thank him for his loving kindness and patience in dealing with my stubbornness. And interestingly, I said I needed to learn, and he took my decision at face value.

Not too long after my commitment, our pastor announced a new Sunday school class for college-aged young people with his wife as teacher. The Lord spoke to me clearly, telling me to ask to be her assistant so that I could learn what this particular age group was thinking.

Pauline, the pastor's wife, was visibly surprised when I offered to help her. This certainly wasn't the norm, for at that time teachers usually had to be conscripted. Terribly embarrassed, I felt very much a stranger and certainly a hybrid, but Pauline graciously accepted my offer, and we had a lovely two years together, a true learning experience as I studied American young people in this class setting.

Travel broke naturally into that sequence, as did Allen's stroke in the spring of 1987. But by the end of the summer, when I heard that the church was looking for a teacher for one of the adult classes, the Lord again asked, "Leoda, what are you doing here?"

"Taking care of Allen," I said, but with a smile, for this had happened often enough to develop a pattern that was easily recognizable. So, little wonder that I approached the person in charge of Sunday school teachers and asked, "Verle, do you have an opening for me?"

He looked surprised, then said, "All the children's classes are filled."

"But I'm not talking about the children's classes," I said. "Aren't you looking for a teacher for the Ambassadors?"

This young man gave me a searching look, then asked, "Are you interested in teaching the Ambassadors?"

"Yes, if you need me. I've taught adults all my life in India. I'd be willing to try."

One of Leoda's neighborhood Bible study classes.

The past ten years tell the rest of the story. Classes in Sunday school on a regular basis, one-on-one discipling sessions, twenty people meeting in our living room on Sunday evenings at times, and six or eight new believers gathered around the kitchen table with Bibles open, many times taking notes. One group of ladies came regularly during the past ten years. We disbanded when I began this manuscript shortly after Allen's heart attack and quadruple bypass surgery this last fall. But we ladies still join at stated times for breakfast, and most of us are in a prayer fellowship that meets each month. We cherish each other, and our study of the Scriptures has greatly enriched me personally.

Whereas the former group mentioned are ladies in their mid-fifties or older, our last small group featured young people from dysfunctional families. To them Allen and I were like grandparents, something they had not known in a Christian context. One had played in a rock band. Soundly converted, he now blesses us with his prayers that bubble forth. Several others came out of addictions, another from a Jehovah's Witness background. The majority have never known a Christian home, but are now determined to give their children one. Two faced persecution at home when, as teenagers, they sought to attend church, and thus raised opposition from family.

But whatever their background, all have been bonded and set free through Jesus Christ, their Lord. They have found a new family! Moreover, they kept Allen and me from growing old by teaching us new vocabulary such as "neat," "cool," and "awesome!" We saw them spring into action when motivated by loving concern. Allen had a heart attack and landed in a hospital twenty miles distant. It was announced in church on a Sunday morning. Four of our small group impetuously banded together to visit him in the medical section of the intensive care unit! Our immediate family had been there and gone since the unit closed at 2:00 for two hours. But the four young ladies got special permission. Two by two, each was allowed five minutes with "Grandpa," and he appreciated their concern and prayer, but told them to "go home and take care of Leoda."

I was resting when the four stormed in, pleased with their success. For the next hour they took over. One washed my feet while another prepared my supper. The other two also found something needful to be done. All of them were helping Leoda! That's involvement, and it had come full circle!

Small groups invite involvement. They also bring people to a valley of decision at times. Many remain with Jesus, but sometimes people turn back. If it happened in Jesus' day, it can and does happen now.

A family who regularly attended our first house church meetings are now in another religion. Another family went to another church, but their young people continued to bring them sorrow. Conversely, by far the majority who have had more than a nodding acquaintance with Jesus Christ as they studied the Scriptures, are now walking with him and witnessing to others.

Is it strange that anyone who seeks to walk with Jesus finds spiritual challenge facing him or her at some point in time? All of us have experienced it. At least, I hope we have, because the Lord Jesus Christ sanctifies all that he touches! Whether it be an empty life, a great sorrow, or some type of pain, he knows all about it.

One of my favorite Scriptures tells me that the Lord remembers that we are dust. I like that, plus the fact that the Apostle Paul tells us that we are merely earthen vessels. And having lived in India where earthen vessels are exceedingly common, and very cheap in price, it is comforting to know that the apostle didn't leave the description there, but mentioned that this earthen vessel which is given to God contains priceless treasure!

What treasure? I believe Paul refers to the presence of God himself living within, bringing light of the knowledge of the glory of God in the face of Jesus Christ. Meaning what? The Spirit of God dwells in these earthen vessels, forming our characters to look and be like Jesus Christ, our Lord. That change goes on throughout a lifetime. Jesus sanctifies all that he touches!

Neighbors and friends are waiting to see the Lord Jesus Christ exemplified in you and me. Let's be true to our calling to know him, and to be made into his glorious likeness. It happens when my will agrees with his, and I say humbly and with grace, "Not my will, but yours be done." That takes more than a nodding acquaintance.

CHAPTER EIGHT

TO THE BEAT OF WHOSE DRUM?

It's Memorial Day, and very soon the parade will be coming down Market Street in Elizabethtown. I quickly finish my task, straighten my dress, and take a quick look in the mirror to be sure my hair isn't untidy. Allen has already gone out to see what is happening.

Ah! There's the sound I've been waiting for—"Dhuka-da-duk; dhuka-da-duk; dhaka-da-duk dhuka-da-duk." As the drum beats sound over the morning air, it announces the fact that the high school band is nearing, and the parade is on its way. I hurry out the front door to stand on the steps of our cottage. From here I'll have a good view. Allen has joined our neighbors and friends gathered at the corner.

Americans love a parade. Another favorite of ours is the Rose Parade seen annually on TV every New Year's Day, originating in Pasadena, California. Allen and I never fail to tune in. Orange Avenue seems so familiar. And, yes, there are those mountains. Our teen-age years rush back with memories, and we watch eagerly for the Salvation Army Band and the Lutheran Hour float. Nor are we disappointed. They are there, year after year with their message of joy and hope. We can depend on them to give a Christian witness in the midst of all the fun and frolic.

In America we find that drum beats usually announce the proximity of a band, either practicing or performing. But my vivid memories of village India projected a far different message than

97

coming for mere entertainment. In North Bihar, where we lived for twenty years and where I also spent my childhood, drum beats announced the approach of some heathen festival! It simply meant, "Come! We're ready to begin." And in response, people flowed toward the sound.

While we were missionaries in Barjora, such an invitation from a neighboring Hindu village penetrated the stillness that settled after the birds quit chattering and went to sleep. I heard a call one evening, "Leoda *Baba*, are you there?"

It had to be old Rebecca, for she alone used the endearing term *Baba* joined to my first name. Being an ancient of undetermined age, Rebecca also belonged to my childhood memories. I hurried out to meet her.

Her frame bent, but her eyes glistening from a still-youthful spirit inside that wizened body, she said, "Leoda *Baba*, hear those drum beats?"

"Yes, Rebecca."

"Come with me to the village if you can. There's something special happening there tonight. You should see it, but I want to be with you when you do. Can you come?"

Apprehension gripped me, but the sound of excitement in my companion's voice made me reply, "Yes, if the Sahib permits. I'll ask him."

After checking with my husband, Rebecca and I were soon on our way to the Hindu village directly east of the mission compound. We talked as we went.

Rebecca explained, "As I said, this is something special tonight, Leoda *Baba*. These Hindus are calling on their gods to take control of them. I want you to see it."

"Oh! What do they do?"

"You'll find it very interesting. We'll watch them, but it's better if they don't see us, so we'll slip into a cowshed nearby. We'll be hidden in the darkness."

My heart seemed to skip a beat as I wondered whether I should have come. She continued, "Hear those drum beats? Hear how fast they're going? That means the crowd has gathered, and the dancing has begun. Come, follow me. Now we won't talk."

We were soon leaning against a wall as we peered out upon the scene brightly lit by flaming gas lamps. Some fifty feet from us, villagers sat on their haunches in a wide circle, the women singing in a high whine to the clapping and the rhythmic beat of the drums. An inner circle of perhaps a dozen men danced, leaped, and cavorted around a tall pole planted in the center of the large open area. The tempo of the drums kept accelerating.

I sensed the excitement, and found the sound of shrill voices, the clapping, and the drum beats almost overpowering, certainly hypnotic. I drew a deep breath.

Rebecca whispered, "When the gods come, the men in the middle will begin babbling with other tongues. That's the sign, Leoda *Baba*. But remember, this is *satanic*! It's not from God! This is a counterfeit. Tell me when you feel you've seen enough."

I pressed her hand in affirmation. Young and brash, I felt sure I could see it through, and during that first ten or fifteen minutes, I did indeed find myself resisting. But then curiosity changed; I began to feel drawn in, even desiring to become part of it all. A warning voice within said clearly, "Leoda, it's time for you to leave."

A quick pressure on Rebecca's arm, her grasping my hand and leading me out saved any further sense of desiring to be involved in a satanic orgy, but the incident troubled me for days. Why wasn't I a strong enough Christian to resist? Actually, I asked Rebecca that question on the way home.

She answered, "You are young, Leoda *Baba*, and I am old. I have had many more years in which to get spiritually strong through testings and trials. Even when I was the only Christian here, I took my stand against all these festivities. Yes, people know me and fear me because my father, too, was strong. We are warriors!"

She continued, "I wanted you to see this, but I knew I must help you. Don't ever forget that the devil's power is very great. Don't ever underestimate it! Keep close to God. God is greater! Don't ever forget that."

I learned one of my greatest lessons that night, particularly precious because shortly after that Rebecca went to be with the Lord. I was with her in her little mud hut. I held her hand that last night and talked to her about Jesus. Her only son, Isaac, was pastoring in

Begu Sarai, about a hundred miles south. In his place, I felt it a privilege to be with his mother when she left this world.

"You are going home soon, Rebecca," I said.

She nodded, her mind clear, her eyes filled with joy. I prayed with her, as did my Indian colleague, preacher Arthur Singh who had called me in response to Rebecca's request. This dear saint of God slipped away from us about a half hour later. Her long battle had ended. She had lived as a warrior for God, and now she went home in triumph.

"I'll tell the *Sahib, Memsahib*." Arthur volunteered. I looked up rather startled. Should I stay?

"Yes, *Memsahib*. I'll send my wife to help prepare the body for burial. She knows how. Perhaps you had better wait on the verandah in the moonlight, since I should take the lantern."

The moonlight helped, and Rubis returned with the lantern, but the entire circumstance seemed very eerie. To work with a dead body by lantern light at midnight is an experience forever etched on my memory. I had never helped prepare a body for burial, but both Rubis and I knew that we dare not wait until morning because of the intense heat. Indeed, shortly after dawn, before the sun scorched the hot earth, Allen and a number of Christians, who had willingly labored to prepare a box and dig a grave in the corner of Rebecca's immaculate garden, laid her body to rest. Nearby stood the church and mission compound that her prayers had brought into being. She was a true warrior for Jesus!

Several years passed, during which time I gave the drum beats a wide girth. But one day our Muslim houseboy came to me and said, "*Memsahib*, they are going to test Lakhu today in the Hindu village south of us here."

"What for?" I inquired.

"He wants to be the priest of this new temple the villagers are building…"

"How can he do that?"

With a wide smile, Haiyun said, "Lakhu claims that Hanuman, the monkey god, comes into him, *Memsahib*. So they're going to test him today, and I'd like to see it."

"Oh? What do they do?"

"I've been told he has to pass three tests. He must climb a greased pole, and walk on coals of fire. Finally, he is expected to stir boiling milk with his bare hand and not be burned. Wouldn't you like to go and see it, *Memsahib*? I'll go with you."

I was curious, especially since Lakhu had worked on our compound as a day laborer. If only Allen was home to go with me, but he had gone away on mission business, so I would have to find an alternative. My previous experience had taught me that the devil's power is extremely seductive, and I remembered dear Rebecca's words. Would this be a chance for Christians to test the power of prayer over idols? If so, we must take it.

So I smiled, and said, "Both of us will go, but first I'll send a message to the Christian village. Any ladies who want to join me should meet me there when the drumming begins. We'll sit together and pray. Haiyun, do you believe that our God is greater than any Hindu god?"

"Of course, *Memsahib*!"

So once again I went to a Hindu village in response to the drum beats. However, this time the sun shone brightly, and we were glad to place our mats in the shade. A half-dozen or more Christian ladies sat with me, and we prayed silently that the power of evil would be broken. We knew our God could do it!

With the accelerated rhythm of the drums, Lakhu came out as though in a trance. Two helpers brought him first to the greased pole standing in the courtyard. He tried to climb the slippery tall bamboo, but slithered down several times. Everyone watched intently, aware that the candidate wasn't performing very well. To cover his deficiencies, two men lifted him by his elbows and practically carried Lakhu over a trench filled with ashes rather than embers. The crowd murmured, and all of us Christian ladies prayed silently but fervently that God would get the glory.

Haiyun, the Muslim young man who sat near us, watched every detail carefully. Noting that the other two tests were similarly unsuccessful, he began speaking boldly to the crowd. "Your idols have no power," he declared. "The God of the Christians is the true and living God."

We ladies left that meeting elated that the Lord had witnessed to himself through the lips of a young Muslim who had been influenced by the gospel of Jesus Christ. Yet in the years that followed, I shied away from Hindu shrines and temples. To me, they represented demon worship, not tourist attractions!

Years later, when living in Bangalore, South India, Allen and I were working with the Far East Broadcasting Associates of India. One day a number of staff, all Indians, went on a picnic to Whitefield, a town some fifteen miles east of our city. It was particularly famous for the palatial residence of Sai Baba who claimed to be an incarnation of Jesus Christ. His disciples came from every strata of society, both from India and abroad. Thousands upon thousands of devotees regularly gathered in Whitefield and other religious centers for a *darshan.*

· What is a *darshan*? Far more than merely viewing or meeting a great man! It implies that the visitor has a life-changing encounter such as Isaiah, the prophet, records when he saw the Lord, "lofty and exalted, with the train of His robe filling the temple" (Isaiah 6:1, NASB). He had a *darshan*—a confrontation that produced a personal transformation, clearly recognizable in his later life and service.

Isaiah's vision of God was genuine, but there are many counterfeits. If you see the counterfeit, you can guarantee that God has made the genuine! Counterfeits are master-minded by the one whom Jesus Christ called "the ruler of this world" (John 12:31, NKJV). More commonly he is known as Satan, or the devil. Desirous of worship and praise, Satan counterfeits the power of God. We read a great deal about him in the Bible, and his wiles are all around us. The Lord Jesus Christ characterized him as being a murderer and liar, and the father of lies (John 8:44).

Living in a land like India, any follower of Jesus has personally experienced the insidious temptations of the great counterfeiter. Spiritual darkness is everywhere. Gurus, swamis, and "holy men" abound, claiming great powers and authority. Sai Baba is one of them, pronouncing himself to be Jesus Christ! To authenticate his claims, he pulls diamonds out of the sand, ashes from thin air, and performs many other miracles which gain him an immense following. We became aware of Sai Baba's impact during our last years in Bangalore and New Delhi. He is literally adored and worshipped by hundreds of thousands, perhaps millions. Not all are Indians; many come from foreign lands.

Now, back to my story. On the day that many of our staff visited the town of Whitefield, fifteen miles from Bangalore, I went along with a two-fold intent—to enjoy fellowship with them, and also to be "light" and "salt" as Rebecca had been for me in a time of testing. Perhaps the Lord would help me to strengthen others.

We traveled by train to Whitefield Railway Station, then walked to places of interest in and around the town. We soon passed Sai Baba's headquarters, a massive compound of manicured gardens and palatial dwellings rumored to having been financed by a wealthy American devotee. Immediately some of the staff showed interest and desired to go in to see for themselves. "You may go," I said, "but I will stay outside and wait for you."

"Oh, come on, Auntie. It's nothing but a tourist attraction! Everybody goes."

"Sorry, my dears, but I'll set a precedent today then by not going. I'll stay here and wait for you if you wish, but I won't enter that gate."

"Hmmm..." someone said. "I'd like to know why Auntie feels so strongly about this. And she's an American!"

"You thought all Americans are gullible?" I asked with a smile. "You forget that I was born in India and have lived here longer than any of you. Maybe I'm not really an American."

"Well—if Auntie doesn't go, I'm not going," someone said, with the result that none of the group went. Had I spoiled their day? I wondered, but as the hours passed, I sensed a deeper bonding between all of us. We sang as we walked, ate our picnic lunch together in a beautifully-kept Christian retreat center, and came home refreshed in the Lord. That day I learned anew that words are meaningless if not accompanied by consistent actions, but that impact hits hard when words and actions synchronize harmoniously. My companions got my message that day which said loud and clear, Why go after counterfeits when one owns the true treasure in one's heart? And I ask, who can adequately estimate Christ's true worth?

Indians love gold jewelry. Indeed, it is standard procedure to provide the bride with expensive twenty-two karat gold sets of necklaces, bracelets, and matching earrings in the dowry. Fourteen karat gold, the norm for jewelry in America, isn't even considered. And precious stones are sought out for the favored recipient.

Even metals of lesser value are kept shining clean. Brass plates, often used for eating, shine like gold. Even though ordinary cleaners which we consider essential aren't readily available to the Indian housewife, she knows that mud with a dried squash "sponge" or even some grass will keep brass vessels shining. In India I learned a secret for cleaning silver. We used toothpaste! Try it. It works.

In India, bridal *sarees* shimmer with gold threads woven into the fabric, which in itself is genuine hand-wrought silk. Particularly in Bangalore, I marveled at the exquisite adornment and attire when ladies went shopping in bazaars. At home they would likely wear everyday clothes, but not when they went out in public! They knew the genuine from the counterfeit, and they enjoyed wearing it.

When I went to Bangalore as wife of the Director of FEBA India, I quickly learned that the ladies on staff wanted me to look the part! But we had lived in Delhi where the hot weather made cotton sarees acceptable. Not in Bangalore! Very soon dear Indian sisters began giving me beautiful silks, and I learned they were pleased when I conformed to the social patterns observed there. So I did my best, remembering that my Christian witness was and should be the deciding factor.

When we retired in 1981, I brought some sarees with me, but most of the time they hung in my closet. To wear them here seemed meaningless. Had my face been brown instead of white, sarees would have held purpose. But to see me in western garb surprised our first Indian visitor, a young man from Delhi.

"Auntie," he said, "I thought I would find you wearing a saree. I don't think I've ever seen you in western dress."

"Cecil, thank you for telling me," I responded. "I like sarees, you know, but now that I live in America, if I wear them people think I'm in costume! You see, if I looked Indian, it might be different, but I'd better be an American while I'm here. Am I wrong, or right?"

It's one of those grey areas, where "black" and "white" merge into something acceptable. America seems prone to such adaptations. Grey areas abound, muting a distinct sense of holding values that are non-negotiable. And that's wrong!

For my purposes, a "non-negotiable" is some truth or standard of conduct clearly stated in Scripture. The first that comes to mind is the structure of the Trinity. Structure is the opposite of fluidity or adaptation. And God holds to structure, even though his methods of working contain much diversity. The Godhead has in it, first and foremost, the Father, secondly, the Son, and thirdly, the Holy Spirit. The Trinity Is Three-In-One, not three separate gods! That's a non-negotiable! We know the Godhead maintains separate responsibilities, for the Father wills, the Son performs that will, and the Holy Spirit applies the work of the Son to every believing heart. But in character they are one, in purpose and vision, one. We have one Godhead, not three. Why? Because this is the way it is!

Another non-negotiable is the way to heaven. All of us would like to make this fluid enough to suit our own purposes, but we can't! If we wrote the "gospel according to Bill or Sue, etc." it would read far differently than John 3:16, which states God's way for going to heaven. Our version would include perhaps our father's religiosity, or ours. Giving to charities would rate high, and certainly, trying to do the Ten Commandments!

Wrong ticket! We are trying to change a non-negotiable! God's ways aren't ours. Besides, he not only originated the plan of salvation, he saw it through. It is a completed fact. Christ died for your sins and mine on Calvary, and when we accept that finished work of God, we are forgiven and made new. Eternal life begins here and now. Membership in God's family is given to every one who repents, and turns by faith to Jesus Christ's sacrifice on the cross. This is God's way, friend. There is none other, for we are dealing with a non-negotiable.

God's plan is simple but profound, for it calls for personal response to complete the transaction. We're not preprogrammed robots, made to act in a certain way. No! We're made in the likeness of God, each with a will of our own. We have the right to choose, but we do not have the right to determine the results of those choices. Those are set. Let us remember, however, that all heaven bows low to hear us whisper, "Yes!"

Dr. Billy Graham adds two simple words at the conclusion of every message. Millions have heard him say, "Now, come." He is extending God's invitation, as though Christ is standing and calling, "Come to Me, all you who labor and are heavy laden, and I will give you rest. Take My yoke upon you and learn from Me, for I am gentle and lowly in heart, and you will find rest for your souls. For My yoke is easy and My burden is light" (Matthew 11:28-30, NKJV).

To procrastinate in responding means that our lives remain dry and powerless, regardless of good intentions. Many people substitute church attendance, religious ordinances, and giving to worthy causes. Perhaps Nicodemus was one of these, until he met Jesus. It took that personal confrontation for him to become a new creature in Christ Jesus, born of the Spirit of God. Saul, another Pharisee, observed the Mosaic Law "blamelessly," seeking God's will, but his life didn't change until he had a personal encounter with Jesus Christ on the Damascus Road. After that pivotal experience, Saul became a different person because he met the Lord Jesus Christ.

He had met Eternal Truth! And no longer did he make the decisions. Saul, the Pharisee, became Paul, the Apostle to the Gentiles. He was a true lover and follower of the Lord, and his letters of exhortation in the Scriptures resulted from that devotion.

You see, Jesus Christ is and always will be a non-negotiable. He never changes! When touched by him, we change into a whole new person. The Apostle Paul expresses it this way: "If anyone is in Christ, he is a new creation; old things have passed away; behold, all things have become new" (2 Corinthians 5:17).

Authority is another non-negotiable. I have spoken of structure, God's eternal plan and Christ's great invitation to all who will come. Now let's talk a bit about authority.

There's something about that word that bothers us. We like to be independent, to make our own choices and go our own way. Seldom do we really find people who *never* want their own way. Even from babyhood we learn to say "No!" It is deeply ingrained in the human heart, and is as old as the devil himself. "You will not die," the serpent told Eve when he showed her the tree of good and evil. Satan, in the form of a serpent, that day challenged God's authority and he has been doing it ever since.

Do you know how the Scriptures characterize us humans? Not as lions, or foxes, or wolves, but as sheep! Sheep can't care for themselves. They follow blindly, yet think they are making right choices. Jesus saw the multitudes as sheep without a shepherd. The prophet Isaiah says, "All we like sheep have gone astray; we have turned, every one, to his own way; and the LORD has laid on Him the iniquity of us all" (Isaiah 53:6).

The Lord Jesus Christ characterized himself as the Good Shepherd, and tells us in John 10 that false leadership lives for itself; true leadership gives and gives, even to death. And he says, "I am the good shepherd. The good shepherd gives his life for the sheep" (John 10:11). Going back therefore to what Isaiah said under the inspiration of the Holy Spirit of God, we are like sheep and our sin, or "iniquity," is simply going our own way. We like to make the decisions and "do our own thing"—regardless of consequences.

In any society, that makes chaos. In Manila, Delhi, and many other cities where authority is challenged, red lights mean little or nothing. They are merely machines! So traffic takes the rules into its own hands! Any of you who have experienced it knows the truth of my statement. Interestingly enough, one time in Delhi, everyone did what the rules said. Why? Because a policeman stood on each corner at the main intersections, and one was in the middle directing traffic. Incidentally, all the accouterments for safety regulations were already there—lights flashing, etc. What made the difference? A human being invested with authority!

Structure and authority are a needed part of society, but in the wrong hands they can go awry. In Christ's hands, we are safe. I invite you to join me in marching to the beat of his drum.

CHAPTER NINE

AS TROUBLESOME AS A MOSQUITO!

Have you ever been camping and had a mosquito torment you? We seemed to live with them in India. They swarmed into our mission bungalow every evening, especially in Supaul, a town surrounded by water during the rainy season.

Mosquitoes love swamps and marshy places, and they enjoy newcomers, finding their blood sweet and inviting. At least so it seemed to Allen and me, who fit into that category.

Moreover, these were malaria-carrying mosquitoes. Fever laid the population low, both night and day, and very soon Allen and I were targeted. They got me, but my husband kept free from malaria for seven years, then had such a severe attack that we thought we would lose him, but the Lord answered prayer.

A mosquito isn't very large, but it is insistent, and it certainly carries potential for great harm. So do the everyday incidents in our lives that tend to dominate our thoughts and behavior patterns. What "bugs" you?

I asked that question of perhaps a hundred of my peers who had lived in India or Africa and returned to the States to work or to settle. I share some of those surprising responses at random:

"In the west—pressures, speed, time measured by seconds and minutes, not days and nights. Hence, less time for relationship building."

A lady wrote she is troubled "how to maintain both my lifestyle and practice so that it is culturally appropriate yet mindful of brothers and sisters I knew in India who live in poverty."

That's a big one indeed. Here's another: "American wastefulness and unnecessary indebtedness bothers me. Immorality, broken homes, loose living, and crime..."

It begins to look like a swarm of mosquitoes! What "bugs" you? A friend said, "The openness of immorality—even to the listing of 'life-long companions' in obituaries. At least in India there was some discretion!"

And here's another breed: "In the political arena, the indifference when even a little reaction and activism could protect against some of the developing trends. It seems that immorality and sin don't matter."

These are big, black "mosquitoes." Some are smaller, but just as bothersome, such as this reply: "I'm bothered by the emphasis on eating and getting overweight, as well as by seeing my friends spend money in almost careless ways that are contrary to our stewardship principles."

One friend wrote, "Yesterday, while waiting in the car in a public parking lot, I was angered because a very strange looking young man, with his car door wide open (though parked), was blasting the neighborhood with vulgar rap from his boom box! I nearly made a fool of myself in trying to shame him, but the whole thought of the degeneration of our youth swept over me."

She told about bringing their college-age daughter to a campus where she hoped to attend school. The girl, looking at the young people said, "Mom! They're weird!" Having lived abroad, she was struck by their dress, music, expressions, and looseness of manner.

Botherations can be multitudinous or minute, but they are part of life. To a "hybrid" they often arise out of the cultural differences that loom large when one enters a new life. After finding out what "bugs" us, it becomes time for action. What have you done about it?

In Supaul, North Bihar, we missionaries counteracted by making a large mosquito-proof "room" of netting to hang on the verandah so that we could work at ease in the cool of the evening. We made it low enough to reach the cement floor, and had a "door" through which we climbed. Placing a table and chairs inside the "room," we found we could spend our evenings both profitably and with real enjoyment, since the bright gas lamp that attracted the mosquitoes and other insects hung outside. Allen profited the most, escaping malaria for his first seven years in India. But both our senior missionary and I had already been infected while out in the villages on evangelistic work.

Prophylactic treatment is better than going through the experience and learning the hard way, but very often we are so stubbornly conditioned in our perversities and wrong focus that we resist warnings. Consequently, suffering has to teach us the desired lessons.

My friend Gladys was wise. As an astute and experienced traveler, she realized that two wardrobes would be to her advantage when she lived in Delhi and traveled back and forth to Hong Kong and other Asian cities. Gladys remembered that dress codes differ in Chinese and Indian circles. In the former, modesty decrees high necklines for ladies, but legs may show. Just the opposite from India!

Cultures vary from one locale to another, and that is to be expected. When the newcomer declares something to be offensive, therefore, such comments aren't taken too kindly! This is understandable. Were we to take time to learn the reason behind the system, perhaps we could show greater tolerance; unless, of course, we are dealing with a non-negotiable, something set by God, our final authority.

Followers of Christ are called to maintain a standard of life and conduct compatible with Jesus' way of life. The Bible therefore stabilizes us, giving us access to God's way of doing things—not only by accruing knowledge, but power through his indwelling Holy Spirit! In the 1950s, when faced with the question, "Shall I continue wearing western garb?" I sought biblical counsel. Why change? Personal preference? Our own holiness, or for the sake of others? Paul became a servant of all so that he might win more people to Jesus Christ. After studying 1 Corinthians 9:19-23 for days, I concluded that in God's sight, winning others should be the deciding factor. The Apostle Paul certainly thought so.

Having been appointed to a new area where, insofar as we could determine, a white woman had not yet lived, it seemed wise for me to lay my western dress aside and "go Indian." Although some of my fellow missionaries didn't agree, yet they allowed me the freedom of choice, and I have never regretted my decision.

Moreover, it provided guidelines for future situations. The basic issue is: What is needed to make my Christian witness credible right where I am? How can I best show Jesus Christ to my friends and neighbors?

Most certainly, when God sent his Son to this world to be the Savior, Jesus was born into "soil" extremely different from heaven's glories. To partake of human nature in itself is an amazing come-down for our Lord. His great humbling is spelled out in Philippians 2: 5-11. It is worth memorizing. And we are told that the same attitude of heart is to be found in his followers!

So humility is a precious virtue for the child of God. A second ingredient is a recognition of God's divine plan for one's life. In the Lord Jesus we see this exemplified in different ways, but two outstanding features confront me: (1) his recognition of the Father-Son relationship, and (2) his acceptance of the Son-Comforter relationship. Our Lord knew his niche, and filled it.

Let's consider these two points. The Lord did nothing on his own initiative. In his last great public declaration before his death, he said, "I have not spoken on My own authority, but the Father who sent Me gave Me a command, what I should say and what I should speak. And I know His command is everlasting life. Therefore, whatever I speak, just as the Father said to Me, so I speak" (John 12:49,50, NKJV).

Look at his relationship to the Holy Spirit. He told his grieving disciples, "It is expedient for you that I go away: for if I go not away, the Comforter will not come; but if I depart, I will send him unto you" (John 16:7, KJV).

How could Jesus best help his grieving disciples when they wanted him to stay with them? By doing the will of the Father, making that his priority. Next, he did what only he could do. He became the sacrifice for the sins of the whole world. The Father raised Jesus from the dead, and set him on his right hand in heaven, where now he intercedes for all who accept him. Christ is now our High Priest, waiting for that glorious day when all will recognize him as the Victor over Satan and evil. He is indeed our Coming King! What if he had not followed the divine plan? Where would you and I be?

So, in our desire to witness, let's keep the order straight. Look first to your own relationship with the Lord Jesus Christ. He is the head of the "church" and we are members. He calls us "salt" and "light," and likens us also to "grain." Salt, light, and grain are easily understood. We use these items daily. But we would find it difficult to do without any of them. Salt penetrates, making food palatable and preserving it from spoiling. Light shines into even the darkest place and conquers! And a grain of wheat, when sown into the earth, dies, becomes part of the soil around it to release the life within. This, in turn, multiplies many times over, bringing blessing to hungry people.

That's easy enough to understand. A mother teaches her children every day, giving herself to them—"dying" as a grain of wheat. Who knows what potential the child has? He or she may easily bless the world!

A man on the job comes on time, does his work faithfully, and becomes a trusted part of the establishment. Others are impacted by his life, for he is "light" in a dark place. Who can estimate the final result?

A secretary in the office doesn't join in telling sleazy jokes, doesn't talk against her superiors, and has a friendly smile for everyone, especially the person who seems to need a friend. She is "salt" in her situation, helping to change the entire scene.

This is God's pattern for witnessing. Not very flashy nor eye-catching, perhaps, but I am reminded that Paul told the Corinthians to consider their calling. Not many mighty, not many noble are called, he says and adds, "But God has chosen the weak things of the world to put to shame things which are mighty" (1 Corinthians 1:27, NKJV). That's the way God works!

On our last trip to India in 1989-90, eighteen months after Allen's two strokes, I caught a bronchial infection for which I had to take antibiotics. Apparently too harsh for my system, the treatment resulted in a unique feature for me—I couldn't stand the smell of garlic, onions, or curry powder! Imagine our traveling over

India for a three-month period, and my not being able to eat the food! I lost seventeen pounds and felt great weakness during those stress-filled days.

That in itself would have taxed the patience of any traveler, but added was the fact that my husband absolutely delighted to be back in India again and went through the entire time triumphantly. Even though he couldn't speak for long at a time, he proved to be a marvel to everyone. And me? I dragged along, going with him from one place to another, meeting friends and being lovingly welcomed as "Auntie." All were delighted that we had come home.

I quote now from my journal which we later published under the title, *Window Seat on a Crowded Train*. We were attending the church-wide celebration of seventy-five years since my father established the work. I journalized,

"We wrote ahead, mentioning Allen's disability for doing public speaking, but as in Bangalore, nobody believed it. Instead, they gave him a major slot on the program! We asked Samuel and Moses to consider substituting, but in typical Indian fashion they preferred not to change anything.

"Therefore, during the main session yesterday, Allen spoke a few minutes concerning the establishing of the church among the Santals and his joy at seeing this great crowd of believers.

"I sat on the platform, confused and blank, also feeling half-sick from anxiety, or perhaps the old trouble? Questions plagued me— how long did I have as a reprieve? When would my husband say, 'Now I'll turn it over to my Aaron?' And when he did, what would the Lord have me say? Should I speak in Hindi as several others had done? I used the language fluently for forty years. Or should I utilize English, with interpretation into Hindi, the committee's preference?

"Just in time I heard the Lord whisper, 'The Twenty-Third Psalm, Leoda, in English.' One of the foreign guests said afterward, 'This was just for me.' But it was for all of us, especially for these simple villagers who know much about sheep and shepherds. Its relationship to everyday living in terms of the will and purposes of God transcends cultures and languages.

"What a gentle Lord we have! The Good Shepherd not only spoke to his sheep, but took care of this undershepherd who needed both message and enabling in a very trying circumstance."

Yes, the challenge we face may be either big or small, but the Lord has the answer. He delights to use our weakness as the occasion to pour in his strength, so that he alone gets the glory.

I would class the above incident as a "big" mosquito. Often the botheration is a small matter, like a little mosquito that simply refuses to go away! The question isn't whether things distress a person, but rather, how do we handle it? Another incident comes to mind.

After Allen had his second stroke in 1987, every time we went to church or were among crowds, I felt my husband's hand on my shoulder as though keeping track of me. And I felt irritated, sure that he was curtailing my freedoms. This bothered me to the point that I prayed about it at night when I couldn't sleep.

Then the Lord quietly suggested that I talk it over with Allen and find out why he placed his hand on my shoulder when in public places. We did so, and he revealed that he felt unsteady, and was looking to me for help.

Since he doesn't often reveal his inner feelings, this sharing changed my whole perspective. He needed me to strengthen him in a time of weakness. Now we could face this hurdle of reentry into normal life, and we could conquer it together.

So I suggested that next time I would stay with him for awhile, then slip away to let him pursue talking with friends on his own. We worked at this until he regained confidence in his ability to converse.

On a recent Sunday morning I heard my husband give public testimony over a microphone in church. He told of a current experience that made him appreciate what the Lord Jesus Christ had done for all of us at the cross. When he finished speaking, Allen invited everyone to say with him, "Jesus paid it all." Unsatisfied with the response, he said fearlessly, "Shout it out!" We did, and for me it was a high moment, realizing that the Lord not only enabled my husband to speak distinctly, but also gave him freedom and courage to lead others. That's a victory worth celebrating!

Celebrations follow struggles. In the spiritual realm they come when we not only align ourselves with our victorious Lord, but also keep him central. To keep focused is our herculean task! Why? Attention drifts so easily to circumstances, and that makes us vulnerable to Satan's wiles! He knows that even our strengths can be used to make us fall. The Apostle Paul says plainly, "Let him who thinks he stands take heed lest he fall" (1 Corinthians 10:12, NKJV). I literally learned the truth of this warning in July 1993 and here's the story:

Allen termed 1993 "the year of Leoda." An angioplasty in March began my troubles. In July I broke my ankle, and in October another bronchial attack somewhat similar to what I suffered in India laid me low. We'll begin this incident with my trying to recover from the angioplasty. My doctors instructed me to control all activity by the "toleration level," which simply meant listening to the needs of my body.

That's good advice, but I soon ran into trouble. Allen, having completed thirty years of service with the Far East Broadcasting Company, expected to retire the end of June. But I still maintained the office, plus getting another manuscript ready for the publisher. My days and nights seemed long as I struggled to regain the health I had lost, but I did find that my body could sustain two hours of work if I rested for one-and-a-half hours in between. That became my schedule, with sleeping, resting, and working filling my time.

Allen's excitement at his approaching retirement gripped him, and he began planning a mammoth two-month trip to Oregon, California, and other points by car! My husband loves to drive, finding it relaxing, so the saga ahead appeared to him an exciting adventure. With some concern I watched maps, plans, and lists appear. He would surely expect me to go along.

For over fifty-five years we had worked as a team together. Did that mean that I would have to accompany Allen on this absurd "celebration" of his retirement? We certainly didn't see alike in this matter! In dismay I went to the Lord for the answer.

"Must I go along?" I agonized in prayer, as I sat on the piano bench in our living room.

When I got still enough to listen, the Lord spoke, asking me a question, "Are you Allen's wife?"

"Yes, of course. I have been for the past fifty-six years."

"Then your place is with him. You go where he goes."

Hmmmm...that's telling me straight, I thought. But perhaps the Lord would comfort me with some special verse and let me know I am loved. Let me try. So I asked, "All right, Lord. I'll go, but do you have any special word of comfort for me right now?"

The answer came back clearly in the words of Philippians 1:29. "Leoda, to you it has been granted on behalf of Christ, not only to believe in him, but also to suffer for his sake."

Suffering? I wasn't at all sure I liked that word! What sort of gift was this? Surely not the comfort I had expected, but God's directive was clear. I was to go, and whatever suffering I would meet would be from his hand, and for his sake.

It wasn't easy to accept, but it helped to know that my times were in the Father's capable and loving hands. He already saw every detail, so why worry?

We left by mid-June, taking two weeks to cross the States. Wherever possible, we held meetings, and sold books. Indeed, the money from my books paid our transportation expenses. Allen resisted the desire to go off on intriguing side trips, and honored my request to stick to the main routes where we knew we could find gas, food, and shelter. That helped, as did my husband's concern for my well-being all along the way.

By the end of June we arrived in southern Oregon, where we spent several glorious days with our niece and husband, Dan and Janie Casad. Then, on our invitation, they went with us a hundred miles north for the reunion that was to be held in a Mennonite Church fellowship hall. As the day progressed, we realized the Lord's purposes in Dan and Janie accompanying us.

Relatives gathered from far and near, and our being with them marked the day as specially to be remembered. Allen is the sole remaining member of his immediate family. Parents and six brothers and sisters have all gone, so "Uncle Allen" holds the special love and affection of his nieces and nephews.

Four wonderful hours of fellowship preceded the moment when someone sang out as we walked down the stairs, "Aunt Leoda, are you all right? Should I help you?"

"I'm fine," I replied. "I have my cane."

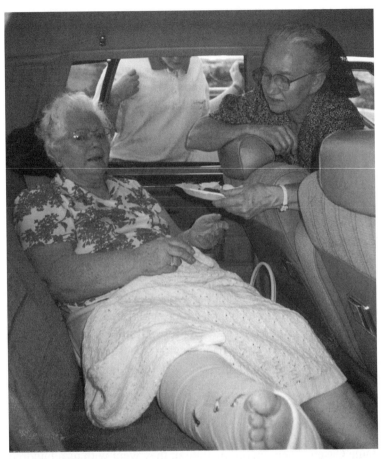

Leoda and her broken ankle.

But within moments my arthritic knee gave way, and I fell on my right ankle. I knew immediately I was in for serious trouble, and indeed this was true. The ankle fractured on both sides and turned! As sympathizers crowded around, I said quietly, "I'll need a wheel chair."

Believe it or not, within two or three minutes a nephew produced one. That in itself seemed a miracle. I confess that the rest of the day remains somewhat hazy in my mind, but I know that Dan and Janie, along with Allen and one of the nieces, took me to a nearby clinic, then to a hospital in Roseburg where the medical staff put my leg in a temporary cast. They would have admitted me for surgery, but Dan and his wife asked that I be transferred to either Ashland or Medford, both towns near where they lived. Since they were residents of Oregon their request was granted, and we traveled that hundred miles southward with Dan at the wheel, and Allen helping me in the back seat. The surgery took place the next morning in Ashland Community Hospital, despite it being Sunday. Thus, I found myself in the center of the New Age Movement in Oregon!

How did I know? One of my nurses had received her name change in India at Hardwar, and was intrigued when I told her the meaning of her name and something about Hardwar, a famous pilgrimage spot in North India. My roommate, a lady about my age, came from a retirement home and was visited often by fellow retirees who were excited about a mutual friend who had a "spiritual experience." She had contacted a new channeler! During my five-day stay in the hospital, I soon learned that to these New Agers, India was like Mecca or Jerusalem. And I had spent over fifty years there!

Somewhere in the haze of awaking after surgery, the whole situation caused me to laugh. I looked up to my heavenly Father and said, "So this is the gift you have given! Father, it is good!" I seemed to see a white sheet of paper on which were the words, "Leoda—July—Broken ankle—Ashland Community Hospital."—and I knew it was no accident!

My thoughts went something like this—"Father! you sent me here, and you are in control. I certainly don't feel like preaching, but please make me sensitive to these hungry, hungry people."

Later I learned that the entire town celebrated Independence Day with a parade and other festivities that carried overtones of Eastern mysticism. One ad in the local paper said, "His Holiness Khenpo Jigmey Phuntsok is an extraordinary Buddhist master directly from Tibet. It is Ashland's good fortune for Holiness to give the Long-Life-Blessing and *Phowa* Transmission and teaching at...." Time and place, and a hefty admission fee followed, with a telephone number provided for gaining further information.

Our Oregon stay stretched to four weeks before the surgeon allowed me to travel again. Visits planned for Washington State and Canada were now replaced by valuable family times and fellowship with Dan and Janie's Christian friends. Perhaps that month's exposure with the Casads had something to do with their now serving in West Africa as support personnel in a leading mission! I would like to think so.

Also, I think back to that experience with joy, remembering that in the midst of the suffering, I learned anew the Lord's gracious enabling. And yes, we did find a "bridge" to hungry hearts through the books I had written. Yannie, my nurse, loved to read novels and was thrilled to receive a copy of *Manorma*. My roommate Elaine, who disdained novels, said she liked travelogues, so she received *Window Seat on a Crowded Train*, as did the surgeon. That busy man, bless him, promised to read every word! Perhaps some day my Lord will share the long-term results of our little Oregon episode.

Home again, after the completion of that 9,000-mile saga under such difficult physical handicaps, I was again faced with on-going commitments. Could the Lord use my weakness? Graciously, he does so.

CHAPTER TEN

WHAT HAVE WE TO GIVE?

My Chinese friend, whom we'll call Tess, stands tall and poised. She dresses well, has good manners, and is very friendly. Tess came to America from the Middle East about seven or eight years ago, bringing with her both sons and daughters. She arrived, commissioned by her husband to provide the family with a quality American education while he served overseas for his country. She knew neither English nor anything about Christianity, and would have faced this formidable task with less courage had it not been for the help of Christian people. As a result of their kindnesses, Tess accepted Jesus Christ as her Lord and Savior, and now carries a prayer burden for others, especially those of her family.

One day this beautiful Chinese lady asked me if we could have one-on-one Bible study. I consented, and soon learned that my new student, though struggling to communicate in a second language, one she was yet learning, certainly displayed good breeding and possessed high mental acumen.

Several years after she arrived in the States, Tess's husband died while serving at his post of duty. Understandably, the new widow's burdens and responsibilities often overwhelmed her. While sharing with me in English as best she could, she said over and over, "I am so weak!" She wiped her tears that kept flowing, and I felt deep compassion.

What did I have to give? Tess needed a friend who understood. My background was different from hers, and I knew no Chinese.

Where could we find common ground? As I heard her reiterate, "I am so weak," the Lord showed me the bridge. "Tell her what to do with weakness," he said.

For me it was a new lesson, one which I was learning in my life as a handicapped individual. Was this the reason the Lord was taking me through his workbook? Well, the directive called for obedience, but first I must find an illustration which Tess could grasp.

A healthy philodendron plant sat on my desk. "Come, Tess," I invited, "let's look at this, and you tell me what you see."

"It's nice...so strong...lovely dark, green leaves."

"Thank you. The leaves are dark because it doesn't get direct sunlight. But did you notice the soil?"

She looked startled, and I continued with a smile, "We don't bother to look at the soil, so don't feel badly. The plant needs soil, but it is out of sight, and the pot isn't anything special, either. It's the plant that gets the attention. And that's as it should be. This is a parable; let's talk about it." What I told Tess that day went something like this:

The soil is like our weaknesses, sometimes called infirmities. In other words, it's rather poor soil, needing the enriching and building up that only a knowledgeable gardener can give. One who loves plants knows what nutrients are necessary and how much water, light, and personal attention each plant needs. With such care, the result will be beautiful!

Place that same seedling into poor soil where the owner goes on guesswork, and the result will be far different. Why should we try to take control of our lives, when the Lord Jesus knows all about us and wants us to come to him with everything?

The Apostle Paul learned this lesson, too, for he knew enough to pray about his troubles, but had to learn that God's answer is sometimes very different than ours would be. Yet, whatever God does is right! Paul learned to give his weaknesses to the Lord Jesus Christ, and the result was a life of joy and victory in the midst of everything. God didn't remove difficulties out of Paul's life; God used them to show his grace! And the conclusion of the entire lesson comes in 2 Corinthians 12:10, where we read:

"Therefore I take pleasure in infirmities, in reproaches, in needs, in persecutions, in distresses, for Christ's sake. For when I am weak, then I am strong."

Tess got the message, and her heartfelt prayer that day more than compensated for the time and effort spent in passing on that which the Lord was teaching me. When we finished our classes several months later, Tess brought me a beautiful flowering African violet, her special thanks for showing her what to do with her weaknesses. It still warms my heart.

Life in the "handicapped lane" taught me lessons I would have missed otherwise. For instance, did you know that furniture is fashioned for normal folks, and not for the handicapped? With an ankle mending after having a double fracture and surgery, I learned that low, comfortable chairs were a test beyond my endurance. Now I looked for a chair with two firm arms with which to push myself up before being able to stand after sitting. Once standing, I couldn't "run" to the front door to answer the doorbell, or grab the telephone when it rang. Now I first had to get my balance, then make my way carefully across the room. And that takes time!

So, small irritations demanded solutions, and my husband and I tried to make life livable. It's at this point that a person often wants to become dependent completely on others, but both Allen and I fought that pattern, with the result that we have been able to remain active. That's a blessing that came with adversity.

When I could no longer take the steps going up to the office, Allen anticipated my need and brought my office desk downstairs. In fact, he gave me the spare bedroom! Bed, dresser, and other items reserved for guests went upstairs into one end of the office. A nice divider which he made gave our guests privacy. One of the first who came after this change took place wrote an appreciative letter, thanking us specially for giving her "space." "Space" in modern parlance means more than just a place to put one's things; it gave her a sense of privacy to be on her own. We have had the same comments many times from overnight guests.

Four years passed. With the house made more convenient to specific needs, neither Allen nor I thought of leaving Elizabethtown for a retirement center. Why would we? Conceptually, it seemed at complete odds with the years of training we had received in India.

Leoda at her desk in Elizabethtown.

My antipathy to the term "senior citizen" has already been confessed. It represented something so completely alien to everything I had known until then. In India, there is no separate "senior citizen" class! The family structure being strong, elders stay with sons in the ancestral home. Daughters get married and go to their husband's family. Hindus, Muslims, and Christians all tend to observe this custom. This cultural practice is based on the strong family system.

Moreover, in Indian thought patterns, years provide maturity, and elders are cherished. The eldest person in the family takes control— Grandpa, then Grandma, then uncles, etc. Young people enjoy a sense of security in this intergenerational setting.

Not only are elders cherished, but male members are considered far more important than females! India is a man's land! Young men defer to older ones, giving a sense of continuity even while working together. Could this provide in part the answer to why India is still very much "there" after five thousand years?

I received my training in India, so I found it deeply ingrained in my mind that an intergenerational society is far preferable to a peer-oriented group based on age, training, or other special interest factors.

Moreover, as one who has lived for Jesus Christ all my life, it bothers me constantly to find the "me" syndrome so very prevalent in American society. Everything here seems to be geared to what makes *me* feel happy, fulfilled, complete! As a result, *I* become the center of my universe, and all of life is supposed to provide *me* with not only creature comforts but beyond that, happiness! Moreover, *I* want it *now*! Fast food services spring up everywhere; instant coffee must be hot; time-saving machines result from an exploding technological quest which strives to keep demand supplied.

Rare are those who laboriously write anything by hand, who seek solitude to meditate on great thoughts. Where do we find a Michelangelo, or aspiring musicians who still prefer to practice long hours in preparation instead of utilizing an easier method? It seems I am one of a rare species—still preferring an electronic typewriter to a computer, a piano to a synthesizer, and a genuine curry to something hastily made out of a tin. Yet I confess, along with my friend in the missionary home in Florida, that such conveniences are nice!

Those of us who hold out against the modern trends are termed "old fashioned" and "not with it." But I remind myself of the like-minded millions overseas who are what I am—a product of my past. They don't know any better, you say, but I remind you of the story in the beginning where the ladies threw the television set out the window because it became offensive to their family values!

Now that's who I am. But, would you believe me when I tell you that in the midst of writing chapter eight of this book, we packed up and moved to a retirement village? Yes, it is true. Even now, as I write, it isn't from the nice office Allen provided for me in Elizabethtown, but from our new home in Messiah Village! By all counts, this should be so traumatic that both Allen and I should be falling apart! But we're not—and therein lies our story.

First of all, to get the record straight, we did not plan to move from Elizabethtown to a retirement center. Why, then, are we here? Were we pressured into making this move? Not really. In broad outline, the Lord Jesus Christ convinced us this is his will and his place for us right now, so we are here and content, praise God.

I've been asked occasionally how to determine the will of God. Allen and I have followed a simple directive through our adventurous journeys and experiences. When three things line up, we move fast: (1) inner conviction, (2) the Word of God, and (3) circumstantial evidence.

This simple little formula has proven itself throughout seven terms abroad, home leaves in between, and our sixteen fruitful retirement years in Elizabethtown. It will continue to prove useful in the days and years ahead.

Now for our story. During the summer of 1995, a young lady asked me to teach her from the Bible. We began one-on-one weekly meetings. By September our group expanded to ten of us around our kitchen table, all brought into the fellowship by one means or another. But one fact soon became apparent—except for Allen and me, all were young and all represented a common past—they had encountered and participated in the effects of non-Christian American society as it is today. Most came from dysfunctional families, one from being a member of a rock band. Several had a history of addictive habits, one was plagued with suicidal thoughts, and all of them needed us! We were Grandma and Grandpa to them.

We became bonded together in Christian love. Open Bibles and hearts produced transformed lives, and we rejoiced. But four days after our sixtieth wedding anniversary, life abruptly changed when Allen suffered a heart attack. Almost six weeks later, having survived a quadruple bypass and pneumonia, he returned home from the hospital.

During his illness we received word from Messiah Village authorities that they had room for us if we wanted to come. When our daughter shared this news, I was amazed—yes, confounded! Messiah Village is a beautiful caring facility maintained by the Brethren in Christ Church. Many missionaries as well as other residents thank God for this haven that caters to the needs of the elderly. It is a half-hour's drive from Elizabethtown, on the west side of the Susquehanna River, about three miles from Grantham and Messiah College. Hundreds of names are on the waiting list! To be approached by the Village at such a time seemed impossible, but it was true.

But I wasn't ready for any drastic move, so I unequivocally said, "No! Not now. One crisis at a time is sufficient." When Allen came out of the hospital, he seconded my vote, and we anticipated two or three years before our names would surface again.

On April 2, 1997, Allen and I sat down to supper as usual. He asked the blessing, but when he tried to eat his soup, his right hand refused to function. It was dead, as was the entire right side of his body. He looked at me and said, "Leoda, I'm having a stroke."

Who but God could intervene? I stood up and prayed a short, fervent arrow prayer—"Dear Lord, stop it!" Then it was time to call family, doctor, life-support unit, ambulance, and very soon Allen was on his way to Lancaster General Hospital. Our daughter and son-in-law went along, but our doctor went straight to church for choir practice and spread the news. Prayer ascended from choir, a Bible study group, and another smaller group that met after the Bible study. When we heard of this concentrated prayer in our emergency, I said, "If you're going to have paralysis, do it on a Wednesday." Rather facetious, I grant, but uttered out of a heart filled with thankfulness.

Allen felt the result of concentrated prayer before even reaching the hospital. He began to move his right foot, and by next morning when he was given a CAT scan, there was absolutely no sign of anything new—only the scars from three previous strokes! Mystified doctors concluded, "A blood clot must have struck and dissolved immediately."

"Yes," my husband answered, "that's what happened."

By Thursday noon I watched Allen feed himself somewhat tentatively with his right hand! For one week he underwent multiple tests. At last the doctors discovered an artery in his neck that was eighty percent blocked. They cleaned it out in an operation, and within another week Allen was home by his own request. All of us rejoiced.

During those momentous days two things happened, one to me and the other to my husband. On April 6, 1997, I went to church as usual on Sunday morning and participated in Communion. Prior to taking the elements, after having enjoyed a meaningful worship service, I bowed my head in self-examination and asked the Lord if there was any hindrance in my heart. He said clearly, "Will you be broken bread for me in Messiah Village if I send you?"

Frankly, I was stunned, but I said humbly, "For you, Lord, I will." On that vow I am living here today.

Thelma, my prayer partner, sat with me that morning, so I turned to her at the close of the service and said, "You'll never believe what the Lord did to me just now."

"What?" she asked.

"In one minute flat, he smashed my will!" I couldn't help but smile at the ease with which the Lord had accomplished this remarkable feat, and I told her, "He asked me whether I would be broken bread for him in Messiah Village, if he sent me there."

She answered quickly, "Oh, Leoda, the Lord just wants your will. He won't send you because we need you too badly here."

My thoughts whirled, and within my heart I knew that the sovereign Lord doesn't waste words. So, one week later I shared the above experience with my daughter and her husband, and told them I was now willing to move to the Village. My time frame, however, would be about a year from then because of commitments. And I gave the matter no further thought.

The day after the Lord spoke to me was Allen's eighty-third birthday. It was also the day he underwent surgery. One of our dear friends took me to the hospital, and before leaving me with Allen, he pressed a card into my hand. "This is sort of special," he said. "Read it, and share it with Allen when he wakes up."

A beautiful, warm feeling of being loved enfolded me when I read that birthday greeting. Allen had drifted into sleep again, so I sat quietly by his bedside and cried for joy. The message said that friends in the church were presenting him with a new VCR as a surprise birthday gift. I knew he would be overjoyed, and I was right, for my husband's eyes shone when I read the message to him later that morning.

We resumed our normal activities very quickly, but before the month concluded, a second invitation came from Messiah Village offering us a nice two-room apartment in the main building. When our daughter told us, it seemed so right. Peace flooded my soul, and although I surmised that this was God's timing, I promised to pray about it, as did my husband. In my private prayer, however, I said something like this: "Dear Lord, if this is from you, please tell Allen. As his wife, I will do anything he feels is right in this situation." Then I waited and watched.

I didn't have to wait long. Lists appeared, starting the whole procedure for another big adventure! Get with it, Leoda, I said to myself with a big smile. Apparently we're going.

A Scripture flooded my mind. When the Lord saved Israel from the Egyptians, they had the assurance of his presence by a cloud over their heads during the day, and a pillar of fire warming the entire camp at night. When they camped, the cloud stood still, yet covering them, but when the cloud lifted and began moving, it was time for the people to move. Then it was that Moses would cry out, "Let God arise!" (Psalm 68:1 and Numbers 10:35). Meaning, of course, that God has arisen and is doing something. It's time we, too, break camp and follow! The analogy is clear—at least it was to me.

I had the inner voice or conviction, now the Scripture flooded into my soul verifying it. How about circumstantial evidence? I waited to see whether, that, too, would fall in line. Sure enough, all of Allen's and my commitments came to a natural end. His had concluded mainly due to his physical problems, but mine continued throughout May, right to the last day. I taught my last Sunday school class on May 25, the final lesson in the course. And I played for a wedding on May 31, the date set weeks before by the bride and groom.

On June 2, 1997, Messiah Village admitted us in as residents. Circumstantial evidence collaborated, and all three necessary items were in place: (1) the inner conviction, (2) the Word of God, and (3) circumstantial evidence. So here we are, praising the Lord with the sense of being exactly where we are supposed to be. Friends, that makes for peace!

Perhaps you are thinking, "That sounds too easy, Leoda. How can any person go against the training of the years, all the thought patterns that have ruled you until now—and within a moment you change so completely?" It's a good question.

To help answer it, let me give an illustration, somewhat analogous to our story. Our nephew, John, has been based in a military hospital near Huntsville, Alabama. We visited John and his family in the early days of their tenure, and found them deeply engrossed in refinishing a lovely old house in a nice community. They renovated both inside and out, including a swimming pool in their back yard. Janet and the two boys joined in wholeheartedly. Moreover, Janet's parents moved from Oregon to Huntsville to enjoy family life.

Already John sensed he might encounter trouble in the future. Could he somehow wrangle an extension to this posting after his term expired? Or should he leave the army altogether? His family enjoyed Huntsville, Alabama!

The years slipped by too rapidly, making the choice obligatory. John appealed for an extension, only to be given a resounding "No." If he remains with the Army, he obeys. The Army wants him in Missouri. His last note gave the answer—they are moving immediately, and their home is up for sale.

Was it merely obedience to a higher authority that brought us to Messiah Village at this time? I think not. It is foundational to give rightful place to the perfect will of God. Jesus did it in the Garden of Gethsemane, but another element touched that obedience into glory. It was the divine relationship between him and his heavenly Father. Love made the difference! And love makes the difference in our obedience, too.

Serving someone you love makes the most tedious task meaningful. Our being here is a delight since we know the Lord wants us here. Yes, there are adjustments. That is always true, but the major question has been settled because we love and serve the Lord Jesus Christ. Jesus makes life worth living, regardless of circumstance. Belonging totally to him brings peace in the midst of storm, and rest of soul in adversity. Relationship is important, but love must crown it all.

In studying the book of Philippians again, I've noticed the beauty and majesty of Paul's relationship with his Lord Jesus Christ. Written from prison, the letter is nevertheless full of rejoicing. Picture the scene: a Roman prison, either in Rome, or perhaps Ephesus; a Roman guard always at hand, and Paul's freedoms definitely curtailed. Under such surveillance he would have many reasons for complaining, especially when some so-called "friends" take advantage of his imprisonment to hold city-wide crusades as a means of furthering their own names!

But Paul's attitude toward his circumstances is simply superb! In humility he writes, "For I know that this [imprisonment] will turn out for my salvation through your prayer and the supply of the Spirit of Jesus Christ, according to my earnest expectation and hope that in nothing I shall be ashamed, but that with all boldness, as always, so now also Christ will be magnified in my body, whether by life or by death. For to me, to live is Christ, and to die is gain" (Philippians 1:19-21, NKJV).

What resulted from Paul's imprisonment? A letter filled with joy! Then, too, the widespread impact upon fellow Christians and the preaching of the gospel with fervor. Even guards in the palace felt convicted, and there were conversions in the royal palace area. Philippians 4:22 mentions that the "saints in Caesar's household" sent greetings. My friend, that's victory!

When we can turn any situation into a cause for giving of thanks, then we're coming close to Paul's directive in Ephesians 5:18-21: "...be filled with the Spirit, speaking to one another in psalms, hymns, and spiritual songs, singing and making melody in your heart to the Lord, giving thanks always for all things to God the Father in the name of our Lord Jesus Christ, submitting to one another in the fear of God."

Can we do that in Messiah Village? Can this hybrid fit in? I think so. We can give of ourselves, our past, and share that which the Lord has done for us as need arises. And a thankful and appreciative heart brings sunshine wherever it goes. Music is something everybody enjoys. My singing abilities are practically nil these days, but I can still play the piano. Perhaps I can share that gift sometimes. But whatever our limitations may be physically or otherwise, a thankful heart is something all of us can share, and a submissive spirit surely brings peace.

I am constantly amazed at life in the Village. Six hundred staff plus volunteers care for the seven hundred and fifty residents. Two hundred of us residents live in independent cottages. Several hundred more enjoy apartments in condominiums, and the rest of us are here in the main building. One dining hall alone caters to over eighty residents three times a day!

This whole complex is truly a community with its own church, three restaurants, a beauty salon, postal service, planned activities, a convenient shuttle service, nursing care, intergenerational functions, security, and maintenance for all. The list grows longer as our perceptions grow, and we recognize the earmark of Christ's caring love over all. I suspect this can be duplicated many times throughout the world, for wherever the love of Jesus touches needy hearts, something beautiful springs forth!

In looking for signposts along this untried route, two words stood out, spoken often and reiterated in letters from friends who heard of our move from Elizabethtown. "Keep writing" they said. Taking that as from the Lord, I made it priority to finish this book. The second directive has come in the many occasions for prayer, so we call this directive, "Keep praying." Allen and I have prayed together each morning and evening for years; now we add prayer while walking the long hallways of this building. The third directive came from my brother, who at this point is in India. When hearing of our move, he wrote, "Sis, don't fall into the leisure syndrome; keep open." For Joe to write at any time is meaningful; for him to send me a two-page handwritten epistle is momentous! I call my third directive, "Keep reaching out." To do this, we are identifying with the Village throughout the week, but have reserved Sundays to go to other churches, and to mingle freely with others so that we don't lose the common touch.

I trust this is helpful to any and all of you who are facing new changes and big adventures. It is making our journey to be what the little chorus says, "Every day with Jesus is sweeter than the day before!"

CHAPTER ELEVEN

TAKE THE ZIGZAG PATH

Since coming to this part of the Susquehanna Valley, we have found some beautiful country roads near Messiah Village. Friends of ours recently took us for an hour's enjoyable ride. In the cool of a summer's evening, we explored some of these intriguing back roads and found the area filled with large homes! "Who lives here?" we asked.

"Probably wealthy people who work in Harrisburg," our driver replied. "Actually, it's only fifteen to twenty miles away from the city...very accessible."

Our tour concluded with a zigzag road to the top of a hill that presented a panoramic view of the entire countryside. It reminded me of another such hill, one near Hendersonville, North Carolina. A friend of ours built a commodious home on the crest, and while visiting them we sat and looked out over glorious countryside, with Mt. Pisgah on the horizon.

Both in Pennsylvania and North Carolina we ascended the easy way—by car up a zigzag road. We couldn't have done it otherwise. Zigzags are there for our convenience. When trying to gain elevation quickly, one might look for a shortcut up the hill, but sometimes physical handicaps make us sit awhile to rest when doing too much. It is comforting then to hear a companion say, "Don't hurry. Take time out."

I recall when Dr. Billy Graham was holding a large crusade in the Coliseum in Los Angeles during one of our early home leaves.

Allen and I were both young and strong, and when we learned that the meetings were attended by thousands, and that the Lord was moving in a marvelous way, we desired to go and take Allen's father. The opportunity came when the crusade authorities announced a special night for senior citizens.

My husband borrowed his brother-in-law's car. Jacob Roth, owner of the vehicle, made sure that the spare tire was in good shape. Then he threw an extra one in for good measure. Our daughter, Joanne, stayed with Grandma while we took Grandpa and Allen's Uncle Will and Aunt Martha to Los Angeles, forty miles distant. Amos and Alice and others came by another car.

The entire experience became a big adventure to Allen and me. He drove very conscientiously, aware of the precious passengers in his care. Moreover, the Interstate highways seemed magnificent after our many years in North Bihar, where most of the time we rode oxcarts, bicycles, a pony, and finally a jeep.

Forty miles in those days was like sixty today. All went well until, on an Interstate, a tire blew out! My husband pulled off to the side, and within three minutes (during which time dozens of cars whizzed by) he had the spare in place. Much relieved, we started on our way again, very thankful that Allen's father had survived that ordeal.

Finding a parking place near the stadium was another stress-filled operation to us "foreigners." But we finally parked, then began walking as fast as we could to the Coliseum. Uncle Will and Aunt Martha seemed to get along fine, but Allen's father lingered. We were concerned when he perched on the step of a parked truck, and took nitro-glycerine (or its equivalent) to get him through this bit of excitement! I remember praying furiously, "Please, dear Lord, I know Father is ready to go home to glory, but please— won't you wait until we get him back in his own house? Not here, dear Lord, please!"

The Lord must have smiled over that prayer! But being a wonderful heavenly Father, he answered and the evening proceeded without further incident. Our elders enjoyed the meeting (made easier for them by the use of the elevator). But on the way home, believe it or not, we had another flat tire! Allen and I rejoiced that Jacob had thrown in an extra. Incidentally, Allen's twin brother,

From left to right: Amos Buckwalter, Allen and Leoda Buckwalter, and Alice Buckwalter.

Amos, passed us and slowed down to see if he could help, but by then my husband had the matter well under control.

In retrospect, we were glad we had taken our elders to that meeting, but we vowed never to do it again, and we have kept that vow. In the meantime, TV offers a zigzag cut toward watching and participating in such activities, too strenuous due to physical limitations.

I recall when I took a "zigzag path" one New Year's Day. Viewing the Rose Parade in Pasadena, California, has always been high priority in our family's life. My cousin and husband live within walking distance of Colorado Boulevard, part of the Rose Parade route. Every year, thousands come the evening before to spread their sleeping bags on the curbs, reserving a prime view for family and friends. We didn't do that, but early each New Year's Day we would drive to Pasadena, park the car at Price and Kathryn's home, then walk to the parade route.

One year when we came back from India, Price and Allen climbed up on the marquee of the office building in which Price worked. From that perspective they took prize pictures of every float and entry. Allen's were so clear that by buying a taped record of the parade, we were able to take back with us a "professionally produced" evening's entertainment!

I couldn't climb the marquee, so I stood on the lower rung of a step ladder that Price carried for that express purpose. That was my "zigzag path," one for which I was very grateful.

Zigzag paths are there to help us when the going gets hard. They are not to be disdained, for they make the rough places plain, and in the mountains they provide a way. A lovely poem puts it this way:

> We climbed the height by the zigzag path
> And wondered why—until
> We understood it was made zigzag
> To break the force of the hill.
>
> A road straight up would prove too steep
> For the traveler's feet to tread;
> The thought was kind in its wise design
> Of a zigzag path instead.
>
> It is often so in our daily life;
> We fail to understand
> That the twisting way our feet must tread
> By love alone was planned.
>
> Then murmur not at the winding way,
> It is our Father's will
> To lead us Home by the zigzag path,
> To break the force of the hill.
>   (Anonymous)

Halfway around the world are zigzag paths with which I am very familiar. They are found in the lower Himalayas near an Indian bazaar called Landour. These particular paths traverse the mountainside on which Woodstock School is built.

Over four hundred children call Woodstock School "home" every year. Its boarding facilities for kindergarten through high school cater to the needs of boys and girls who are preparing to enter American universities some day. And this is within a Christian atmosphere! During Joanne's growing up years in India, Woodstock was home to her for nine months out of every year. Along with many other students, she ran uphill from hostel to school, to the library, to classrooms, and probably ran down again! Our young people do that in Landour.

When I speak of hills, I'm not talking about gentle slopes such as we have here in Pennsylvania. I mean mountains, for even the lower Himalayas are known for their steep heights and depths. When one goes to Landour, one can look to the north and see range upon range set in layers, with the highest mountains on the world on the horizon. The twenty highest mountains in the world are found in the Himalayas! These snow-capped giants command the respect of every mountaineer. In comparison to those perpetual snowbound peaks, Landour's hills and valleys appear insignificant, despite the 7,000 ft. elevation!

The letter I received from my brother, Joe, the other day came from Landour. He and his wife own a house—Pennington—near Woodstock School where their eldest daughter, Judy, and husband work on staff. Judy and Dana's children are like mountain goats, scampering up and down trails, never bothering with the zigzags. Like all other locals, they prefer the shortcuts.

But Joe's home, built on a ledge some fifty to a hundred feet above well-traveled Tehri Road, used to have a nice gate, signboard, and zigzag approach—until about one year ago. Then one night, at the end of the monsoon season, with a roar like thunder, the entire front side of the mountain slid down, covering Tehri Road. Had it happened in the daytime, there would no doubt have been fatalities. But God in his mighty wisdom withheld the house and its inhabitants from harm. Nor were any lives lost since it took place at night!

Gone is the gate, the signboard, and the zigzag path to Pennington. Instead, a stone retaining wall now protects the house above, and stone steps lead from Tehri Road to its entrance. Youngsters no doubt love them; I'm not sure about their elders.

No amount of wishful thinking will bring back Pennington's approach and front yard as we knew it. Change has come, inevitable change! And we are reminded that life is that way, too. Somewhere, sometime, change comes, both in us and in our circumstances. Sometimes we are like my poor little African violets.

African violets on the window sill in Elizabethtown.

When we moved from Elizabethtown to Messiah Village, we brought a few treasured plants with us. Three are African violets, with which we had good success in our former home. But here they are struggling. The problem seems to be the amount of light they need. With only one window in which to keep them, for these three months we have tried to help them adjust. "Too much light," said one knowledgeable friend. In trying to protect our plants, the matter of change has been very fresh in my mind. Those African violets loved the living-room window in Elizabethtown. But neither plants nor humans can expect all of life to be as it was before. Change comes! And when circumstances seem too difficult, I'm glad for a loving heavenly Father who takes care of us and our needs.

Consider the magnitude of Moses' task in leading an entire nation out of servility to the Egyptian lords. No wonder Moses hesitated to accept the responsibility! However, Moses had much to his credit when God called him to go to Egypt and ask Pharaoh to release the Israelites. He had lived in the wilderness for forty years, knew the desert routes intimately, and had learned much about caring for his father-in-law's herds which he protected.

Moreover, he was now mature, a very different individual from the young prince who was trained in the highest arts of the Egyptians, but who had tried to protect his people, the Israelites, by "doing his own thing" in his own way! That arrogance changed during those forty years in the wilderness. God was teaching Moses to be a true leader.

Now he was unsure of himself, and wondered how God could use him. His hesitancy in responding to the call of God finally led to God giving him his brother, Aaron, as an aide. But later developments showed Aaron as the weaker of the two men. In fact, Aaron's giving in to the demands of the multitude in Moses's absence caused great trouble and sorrow. Except for one stabilizing factor, Israel's release from bondage and their journey to the Promised Land would have ended in miserable failure. Despite their grumbling and outright rebellions, the people finally reached the land of Canaan because Jehovah God took them by the zigzag path! For forty long years they wandered in the wilderness, learning lessons of trust, laying to rest along the route those who were disobedient to God. Beyond that, they became disciplined to obey God-given leadership as found in Moses, and then Joshua, his successor. Above all, the children of Israel learned that man wasn't in control; the true leader was God himself!

Only when the children of Israel learned those lessons, did Jehovah God allow them to set their feet in the Jordan river. As they did so, the waters parted, and another mighty miracle from their God took them across on dry ground. But remember that forty years of zigzag paths had prepared them for this moment.

You and I are much the same. We like to map out our own routes and follow our own thinking. Often we depend on educational qualifications, books, training, and natural abilities. When we run into difficulties, we wonder why.

We need to remember that neither Moses's training, his natural abilities, nor his past experience could have matched the immensity of the demands placed upon him. The story ended in success only because God was with them! Had Jehovah God forsaken them, they would have known only defeat. They would have been like other men.

Need I point out the obvious? The Lord makes it clear enough in his Word. Time and again we are told there is not one thing we can do to attain his righteousness. Yet despite the love of God and his great plan of salvation, we insist on living life without God in control. Yes, we want the Lord's blessings, but not his Lordship in our daily decisions. So we have to learn the hard way—by wandering in the "wilderness," taking all the zigzag paths because of our disobedience and rebellion. It is part of the learning process.

Perhaps, like the Apostle Paul prior to his conversion, we are full of good works, filled with zeal and desirous to live for God. But something is missing. Like Saul, the Pharisee, are we bypassing Jesus? When Saul capitulated, God transformed him from a Pharisaical Jew into the apostle for the Gentiles. What a vast change!

For you and me also, saying "yes" to the Lordship of Jesus Christ is the key that unlocks closed doors. When he controls us, mountains become a way, bastions crumble, and righteousness rules within. A life lived under the shadow of the Almighty portrays strength and beauty. It mystifies onlookers.

Isaiah, the Old Testament prophet, put it this way:

"Have you not known? Have you not heard? The everlasting God, the Lord, the Creator of the ends of the earth, neither faints nor is weary. His understanding is unsearchable. He gives power to the weak, and to those who have no might he increases strength. Even the youths shall faint and be weary, and the young men shall utterly fall, but those who wait on the Lord shall renew their strength; they shall mount up with wings like eagles, they shall run and not be weary, they shall walk and not faint" (Isaiah 40:28-31, NKJV).

What does "wait" mean? To linger, tarry, abide one's time, to remain with someone or something that holds one's attention. I know a twelve-year-old boy who is consumed with a passion for reading. He carries a book with him wherever he goes. When his elders begin conversation, this lad settles down to reading. When the family goes somewhere in the car, he carries a book with him and unobtrusively gets it out during the journey. Is it any wonder that he does very well in school, or has a grasp of subjects that others don't possess? He has immersed himself in good books.

To linger in God's presence, to rest in his Word, to dwell upon his precepts, to fill one's life with what he desires and wants—perhaps that would adequately express the strength of the term "wait." Those who do this tap into a source and supply far deeper than anyone can express in human terms. The prophet says that such a person will mount up with wings like eagles, will run and not be weary, will walk and not faint. Why? Because the resurrection power of God flows through him!

Not too long ago I watched a television program on eagles, and was interested to learn that they wait for air currents, then soar effortlessly upward with little or no motion of their wings. My heart responded as I thought of this magnificent Scripture in Isaiah. Waiting on the Lord results in our soaring upwards with wings as eagles. What an illustration of living in the glory of the Lord's presence. It takes away the need to struggle, to work hard, to figure everything out. Why? Because God is with us.

I think "soaring" precedes "running"—not only in the scriptural promise but also in daily living. Touching the Infinite has to come first, but running means we're touching ground, living in a real world with real people around us. To be able to "run" is wonderful. Then comes the time when all we can do is "walk." But the Lord is still with us, and takes us through the hurts and painful times as well as through joy, all with an inner strength and radiance that comes from God's touch alone.

This is a marvelous promise! Does it work?

I know it does! Regardless of circumstance, "there is a place of quiet rest, near to the heart of God. A place where all is joy and peace, near to the heart of God!" That is soaring on eagles' wings.

Running? Busy schedules and pressures mount, and from morning to night one sometimes wonders where the strength comes from. We're told it is from God himself! It comes with waiting upon him, lingering in his presence, enjoying his fulness with a passion and obsession such as Michael exhibits with his books. A book is always at hand, yet he lives a full-orbed life such as playing soccer and taking piano lessons!

Can a busy person be absorbed with God? Definitely! With the Spirit of God living within, communion is possible throughout the day, even in the busiest moments. As a person lives constantly in

God's strengthening, others are amazed. "How do you cope?" they ask. Or people look at you and say, "You look so well!"

That comment always makes me smile, because if it is true, it is only because the Lord is pouring in his strength and grace. So the Lord should get the glory!

What about walking? Sometimes one walks briskly, presuming you haven't broken your ankle! Since I have, walking briskly for me seems to be in the past, but not in God's sight. Regardless of the circumstance—even including pain and trouble, either physically or emotionally, and sometimes both at once—the promise of God is still true. When we have him with us, we can walk and not faint. We can make it by the riches of God's grace.

Living now among people who have reached their eighties, some their nineties, and several who are over the century mark, we are meeting some fascinating individuals. One such person came to our door recently as a "volunteer" to welcome us to our new home in Messiah Village. I certainly would never have placed Anna Brubaker in her nineties, but our guest is now ninety-five years of age, walking with a cane since she broke her hip four years ago. But Anna makes it her business to welcome newcomers. She often places the welcome sign on the door, and delivers flowers. Later, as a volunteer, Anna officially visits to be sure all is well. No wonder she is outgoing, full of cheer, and enjoying life. She has an inner dynamic that comes from a daily walk with God.

Meeting her reminded me of another beautiful lady whom we knew prior to our first leaving for India as missionaries. With her husband, Mother Stump lived near Morrison, Illinois, and attended the small country church my husband pastored. In her mid-eighties, twenty years her husband's senior, Mother Stump nevertheless delighted us with her recitations of poetry that she gave often in Sunday school and church. Like Anna, she relished people as much as they loved her. Her cookie jar always held a tempting supply of freshly baked delicacies, with an extra one for her young pastor, Allen Buckwalter.

No wonder she outlived her husband! We visited this remarkable lady on one of our furloughs, and found her in her own home near a campground in Ohio where we were speaking. Mother Stump was now well over the hundred-year mark, but the same cheery smile greeted us when we caught her busy at her sewing machine, making pillow tops! Her cookie jar stood ready, but she apologized that the contents came from the store instead of from her oven. She had learned the value of "zigzag paths."

We mentioned we were speaking in the camp, and were happy to learn that she was nearby so we could meet again. With her chuckle she confessed, "I've been attending camp for years. Each time I go, I'm sure the Lord will take me home before camp time returns, so I stand and say goodbye. But finally..." Mother Stump paused, and laughed.

"Finally, what?" we prompted.

"Bless your heart, my dears, I'm ashamed to go. I've said farewell so many times! I'm sure I would enjoy the meetings, but I'd be embarrassed...so I just stay home."

Mother Stump impressed us younger people, because even at her advanced age, instead of fearing death, she anticipated leaving this room for "another" one! It would be just like walking through the door to go somewhere else, and after awhile the others would also join her. Is she quoting recitations in heaven and delighting the hearts of her hearers? It surely is possible. And someday we will know.

I doubt that Mother Stump realized how much she blessed us. However, that didn't alter the fact that her life seemed a fragrant sacrifice of praise to God himself. Can we learn from her example?

CHAPTER TWELVE

BLOOM WHERE YOU ARE PLANTED

While sitting under a hair dryer in the beauty salon the other day, I learned a lesson. A window near me looked out on a shaded patio, and on the window sill at my elbow sat a beautiful African violet in full bloom. I marveled at the wealth and richness of those purple blossoms.

Then I saw the tree outside, providing shade not only for the walks and patio at that end of the courtyard, but also for my little sensitive friend inside on the windowsill. And I said to myself, Leoda, you are like that violet. The brash sunlight is far too glaring for you, but your God, the Almighty One, comes between you and all that is harmful. He is with you to shield you; he has taken your hurts and your pain. When he transplanted you from India to America, *he* came with you and you remain in his caring love through every circumstance. Don't have a worry—just bloom, bloom, bloom!

You may place your name there with mine, and be encouraged. Whether our stories match or not is immaterial. All of us experience change with the passage of time.

Summer has gone, and schools are once more filled with students. Weather forecasts call for cooler nights, a reminder that casual clothes will now be replaced with layered and more formal clothing through these autumn days. Beach parties are forgotten, and plans for trips northward to see the autumn leaves are afoot.

Then comes the annual preparation of the R.V.'s for the migration southward to warmer climes to escape winter's onslaught!

Seasons come, and seasons go, bringing with them attending agendas that fill our days. When we can take a break from our busy schedules, we sigh and reflect that time is going too fast. Where has this week gone?

Have you ever felt you would like to turn the clock back to "the good old days"? Life seemed so much simpler then, but did we ever have more than twenty-four hours in our day? Have we conveniently forgotten the unpleasant and retain only those memories we enjoy? This may be true for most of us, and indeed this may be a blessing in disguise. For both good and bad mingle in life's experiences to guide our footsteps into safer paths.

Life is a journey, a path that cannot be retraced. Even as night follows day, and weeks, months, and years brings physical changes for each one of us, so we must remember this word of hope: Today is mine! "This is the day the Lord has made. We will be glad and rejoice in it!"

"Today is mine!" That's what a young man we know must be thinking as he begins trekking northward to Pennsylvania on the Appalachian Trail. Yesterday he attended church services in Elizabethtown. He spent his summer walking southward from Maine. Now he has flown to Georgia to walk northward. What an endeavor! He will get the full benefit of the autumn's changing colors, and will no doubt arrive back by Christmas! His will be a journey to remember.

We had one such memorable journey in India by motorcycle that can never be repeated, but will never be regretted. Allen and I traveled from Delhi to Agra, Nagpur, Bombay (now called Mumbai) and northward through Gujerat to Rajasthan and back to Delhi. We did it early in our fifties, traveling on an English motorcycle. It took us a little over a month. Leaving at the end of the monsoon, we arrived back in September, having experienced a dream come true. Here is our description, written in December 1962:

"Winding roads through rolling hills lush with the green of the monsoon—ancient forts built on hilltops silhouetted against a backdrop of fleecy clouds—endless ribbon of road leading through hill and dale, checkered farmland and teakwood forest—peacocks calling from the fields and woods—gaily answering the schoolboys, yell for yell—ah, yes, roasted peafowl dinner and Chinese supper—talking radio and sharing mission and church problems, and joys—making new friends and renewing acquaintances—lunch on a hillside under a lone palm tree, or picnicking on a sandy beach with friends at sunset—from charming villages of tribal peoples in remote jungles to the sophistication of great cities—from teeth-chattering roads through rugged mountains to floor-smooth cement roads leading to tourist attractions—always God's umbrella of heavy clouds overhead threatening rain, but dry ground underneath so that we could travel safely!

"And what more can we say of the warm hospitality we received everywhere—the willingness to help—the interest in radio evangelism—prayers and best wishes of friends all along the way—a dream fulfilled, to remain a dream forever."

Yes, we'd do it again, if we could turn the clock back! But since we can't, we're glad we traveled over 2,400 miles, contacting fifteen different missions and organizations, and telling them about radio work which was then a new arm of missionary effort. This promotional tour took Allen and me five weeks. I lived out of a seventeen-inch suitcase, had two changes of clothing, plus two sarees. It took six months of planning and less than ten minutes to repack each time! We drank boiled water, carried our lunch each day, and spent nights with either Indian Christians or missionaries. Consequently, not having to buy anything from bazaars, we stayed well. It was the trip of a lifetime because we did it when we could.

An eleven-year-old boy learned something about life's journey from the great Indian Christian, Sadhu Sundar Singh, a convert from Sikhism, who tramped India's villages preaching the gospel of the Lord Jesus Christ. One day the *sadhu* (holy man) arrived at a preacher's home in Ladakh, way up on the borders of India and Tibet. He desired to penetrate new territory and was headed for the forbidden land of Tibet. Ordinarily the Lal family would have rejoiced, but today they were grieving the loss of their father. At this crucial hour in the lives of these lone Christians, the Lord sent the *sadhu* to personally minister comfort.

Kenny Lal, eleven years old, stood on the verandah, wiping tears that would not stop. He gazed long and hard at the mule trail that led past their home and disappeared when a mountain hid it from view. The boy reflected that this is like life's journey. It abruptly comes to an end.

His heart ached inside his breast because even now his father's body was being prepared for burial, and Kenny had been told to stay out of the room. Life seemed hopeless and he hastily wiped a tear away when he felt a hand on his shoulder. A male voice somewhere behind him said softly, "What are you thinking, my son?"

It had to be the *sadhu*. Kenny whispered, "Life is like that road—it ends."

The voice full of compassion, replied, "You are partially right, my boy. Life is like that road but it does not end abruptly as it appears. It continues on around the mountain and leads into another country."

That quiet talk between a man of God and a young boy made a pivotal change in Kenneth's life. "The *sadhu* told me about heaven and how to get there," he said in recounting the story to Allen and me many years later in Delhi. Had the *sadhu* waited for large crowds, bypassing this lonely, grief-stricken lad on the cottage verandah, the story would have been very different. Sadhu Sundar Singh was being particularly Christ-like in giving himself to those whom he touched. And for this one boy, as for many others, it meant a new beginning, a glimpse of what lies beyond the curve in the road—abundant *life* in Jesus Christ.

Many a godly person has ministered to me in my times of need. Such contacts are often unobtrusive, but very meaningful. To "bloom where planted" doesn't require a platform and thousands of listeners. It seldom is that! More often, it is like my gentle little African violet on a windowsill, blooming in the shade of a protecting tree outside its domain. Many a saint quietly lives out the power of resurrection life, bringing both solace and joy to hungry, searching hearts.

But there are those who enjoy doing things in a noisy, big way. Jesus doesn't bypass the Simon Peters, either! Indeed, he incorporated his particular Simon Peter into the inner three. Much of Simon had to become "Peter." The big fisherman must have loved adventure, challenge, and the spectacular. If I'm not mistaken, he's the only one who requested Jesus to command him to also walk on the water, thus proving that Jesus wasn't a ghost, but actually their living Lord! What did Jesus do? He said one word, "come!"

I think our Lord must have smiled at that request—it is so very human! We love the spectacular. We run after spiritual experiences which "prove" that God is here. He said he would be, so why panic? But instead of trusting when we cannot see or understand, we seek some "sign." Often, our patient and loving God gives it to us. He is indeed gracious.

Simon's request was granted, and he walked steadily on the water until he began to look at the wind and waves, and not at his Lord. Then, sinking, he called loudly for help, and the Lord lifted him up. Does this sound familiar? Too often, your life and mine is very much like Simon's story—we vacillate between trusting and doubting, and the Lord smiles patiently, waiting for us to trust.

I don't sense the Lord commending Simon for asking to walk on water—to have a miracle. Instead, he expected Simon to be able to do it, if this was his desire. Yet, when Simon began to sink and desperately called out for help, the Lord lifted him up and asked, "Why did you doubt?"

The story ends appropriately by Jesus and his disciple getting into the boat, the wind ceasing abruptly, and the disciples worshiping Jesus. What all of this says to me is that we cannot manipulate God to provide a miracle when and however we desire. It is *his* prerogative to allow the wind to blow hard, to let the waves threaten us. But, if that be the case, you and I are still as safe as when the Lord and we are in the boat and the sea is calm!

To rightly analyze this amazing story, we should take it in the context of its preceding event, the feeding of the five thousand. Talk about emotion! The disciples had helped by distributing the loaves and fishes to that hungry crowd. They knew their Master had multiplied it from the simple little gift brought by a boy who believed it might help.

These two incidents, coming one after the other, make sense when we read in John's account that the people wanted to make Jesus King, and tried to take him by force. In Matthew's Gospel an additional insight is added—that Jesus dispatched his disciples *before* he sent the crowd away. That isn't the ordinary procedure for dealing with a mob! (Not unless these disciples were ringleaders in the movement! In which case, the Lord would make them get into the boat and leave first, prior to his sending the rest home.) After a day of miracles, and an evening packed with emotion, Jesus found himself free at last to climb the mountain alone. There he spent the night hours with his heavenly Father, getting his orders straight.

There may be another explanation, but since we're not told all the details, your guess is as good as mine. But whatever the truth is concerning that eventful evening and night, one thing we know—the Lord must be in control. Twelve disciples had twelve different characteristics. Temperaments differed, showing diverse behavior patterns. But whatever the circumstance, harmony, peace, and purpose come only when Jesus Christ is Lord.

Life becomes pretty adventurous at times, with emotional highs and lows, as evidenced in the previous accounts recorded in the Gospels. I wonder what those disciples talked about the next day when Jesus gave them the chance to be alone. Was it admiration for Simon Peter's request to walk on the water? We can be sure that they didn't let Peter forget that he fell. Perhaps they still felt numb over Jesus' refusal to allow the people to make him king. That would be a natural reaction. But I could hope that these men who lived so close to their Lord were somehow touched anew when they worshiped him, and that in the quiet of a new spiritual realization, they, too, were changed.

Life is like a journey; life is like an adventure. In today's world, seeking adventure is "big business." America searches out adventures of all kinds—going on safaris, speedboat racing, surfing, parachuting, mountaineering. Highways and beaches are crowded with pleasure lovers seeking thrills. Sports arenas are packed with thousands upon thousands. The list grows long, often reminding us that living only in terms of one's own selfish desires can become a futile quest.

Fortunately, there are some who truly live for others, accepting a challenge to try to fill a need. To such, life becomes an enriching experience. Cross cultural living does this very quickly, as in the case of teachers leaving our shores. A college girl spends her summer teaching English in China, a young man serves in the Peace Corps in Ecuador, a mature husband and wife team up to be support

Fourth generation M.K.s: Andy and Phillip Crider, sons of Dana and Judy Crider (and grandsons of Joe Smith, Leoda's brother). Their great-grandfather, H. L. Smith, first went to India in 1913.

missionaries in West Africa. These and many others like them are living adventurously while seeking another's good instead of merely filling their own desires. We salute such, and know they will never regret any sacrifice they have made to live abroad.

But we can never bypass the unsung heroes who give themselves daily for the needs of others. They, too, may be living adventurously, forgetting their own needs and desires so that they might help others. Jesus called it "giving a cup of water in my name." He assures us that their reward is coming in full!

This brings us to our third simile: *Life is like a city, town, or hamlet.* We must live in relation to others, and cities, towns, and villages have one common bond—people live there! But people being people, living in relationship with those around us may often be hazardous, leading to ill feelings, conflict and strife, accelerating to all manner of evil. The Bible talks about such. It also describes an alternative—living in peace and harmony with one another by the amazing touch of God. Who wouldn't vote for the second alternative? The Apostle Paul admonishes us saying, "Inasmuch as lies within you, live in peace with all men."

In November 1989, Allen and I visited my favorite city. We traveled far to get there, half-way around the world to India. Darjeeling, tucked away in a remote spot on the northern borders, has a rich background, serving as a hill resort during the time of the British colonizers. Our three-day visit to this idyllic spot in the Himalayas is memorable, for it takes me back to my childhood. I quote from my journal:

"'Ghoom, Sonada, Thoom, Kurseong—all are left behind...' The old school song we shouted out the windows of the 'toy train' on going-down day from Darjeeling became a sing-song in my mind as our taxi climbed those fifty miles of curves from Siliguri to Darjeeling, a city that I love.

"Normally I don't love cities. There have been a few (but very few) exceptions. Small towns, yes! Countryside, definitely, but cities? No!

"Why? Too crowded...too dirty...too uncertain.

"Somehow, Darjeeling stands apart. The 'Queen of the Foothills' as she was called, has stolen my heart. I remember the hint of magic, the touch of the unbelievable as we would turn the last corner to see the city nestled midst pines and rhododendrons. If we were fortunate we would see the snows, a very insignificant name for the third highest mountain in the world—Kangchenjunga, magnificent with its imposing array of satellites! But that's what we called them—the snows. Once their grandeur sifted into our spirits, all other mountains paled. I still measure the Rockies by the Himalayas, as seen from Darjeeling.

"Today is November 11, and here I am, back in my beloved city. My excitement mounted as we entered Kurseong, and our taxi stopped for a welcome cup of tea and a snack. School children dribbled down the road, all dressed in uniforms. Public transport vied and maneuvered to outwit each other, playing chicken. With much honking of horns, we finally cleared the town. The ditty took over and I told my companions, 'Thoom comes next, then Sonada; after that the town of Ghoom, and finally, Darjeeling.'

"But as we neared, I wondered what the years had done to my dream city. And I found it had changed, even as had I. However, the glory of the mountains remained. My dream has ended with the reality of Darjeeling as she is today.

"But those childhood memories are precious—of the time when British lords and ladies made this mountain resort a place for pomp and ceremony. That's gone! So is the Bengali flavor that took over when India became a Republic. Now the local Nepalese population have made it theirs.

"But this city still has personality plus. Natural beauty is here in abundance. I sense an aliveness. The people that throng both the lower bazaar and the Mall look well dressed, thrifty, and purposeful. Why shouldn't they control their lovely city?"

During our three-day visit to Darjeeling, clear, sunny days and warm-hearted hospitality made our time unforgettable. Meeting my old schoolmate caused me to write,

"I'm sitting in the gardens of this gracious hotel that is managed by my former schoolmate, a Tibetan lady named Mary Ladenla Tendufla. An amazing expanse of hills and valleys spreads before me, backed up by the snows. Not the entire range, just the right end—but imposing, nevertheless. To get the complete range, one has to walk five minutes from here to Observation Point. We did it yesterday.

"This place pulls one back into the British Raj—no radio or TV, but fires in the hearth, one-day laundry service, hot water bottles for your bed along with heavy woolen blankets. Our neat, smiling Nepali maids anticipate our every want. Liveried 'bearers' (stewards) wear dark green woolen tunics, trousers, and matching turbans. With white gloves they serve full four-course meals to all of us guests in the spacious dining room that looks out on these majestic peaks.

"Here in Windamere Hotel, time turns back. The world seems far away, paling in the imminence of nature's lavish splendor. Day-old news doesn't seem so important when you can explore trails and breathe deeply of fresh mountain air. You walk the Mall, fingering the finely knit shawls sold by vendors. And there's a comfortable old-world feeling one gains from these buildings. They have matured, weathering many storms, and like old friends, accept you as you are and ask the same in return."

That's the Darjeeling I last saw, a city yet unspoiled by modern encroachments. Or is it? One can never be sure, for new technologies seem to push in everywhere. Do you suppose a computer has found its way to Darjeeling? It could easily be. One thing I know. Darjeeling holds its charm because of those snow-covered peaks. As long as Kangchenjunga shows its face, reflecting the corals, pinks, mauves, and golds of the sun kissing its craigs, this city—regardless of change—will continue to attract those who long to experience the mountain's beauty and strengths.

It seems to me that Darjeeling's story parallels life. It has experienced vast changes politically. Ethnically, it hardly seems part of India, for the general public has come from surrounding mountain kingdoms—Nepal, Bhutan, Sikkim, and Tibet. But it is still in India and remains a favorite tourist attraction for the people of the plains. Indeed, the "toy train" still runs each day from Siliguri to Darjeeling, and by an act of the Indian Parliament will continue to do so. All other steam engines in the country have been auctioned off and put to rest. But the proud little blue engines of yesteryears, considered to be one of the seven wonders of the world, will continue to do their duty each day. These sturdy little mountain climbers have been accorded this great honor by Parliament.

Moreover, change hasn't taken away the city's charm. It has merely matured it. As one local person put it, "This city used to be called "Queen of the Foothills," but now it is "Grandmother." When we remember that age is revered in the Orient, this is a title of honor.

Darjeeling is magnificent! So are the people of God who live in his presence. We change; *he never changes*. We are fragmented without him. In him we have peace. Ethnically, the Lord Jesus Christ unites us, and regardless of background we can sing:

> Amazing grace, how sweet the sound
> that saved a wretch like me;
> I once was lost, but now am found;
> was blind, but now I see.

The people of God, basking in the light of his presence, daily live and know his "amazing grace" that lights up our lives to the point of reflecting that beauty to others. But even as Darjeeling often knows clouds and rain, hiding the great mountains from view, so our lives also know trial, sorrow, and personal grief. But through it all the glorious presence of Almighty God remains with us. We know God is there!

That assurance makes all of life worthwhile, takes away anxiety and care, and helps us to keep on keeping on, irrespective of circumstances. You and I must bloom where we are planted! I thank God that *he* does it in and through us for his own glory.

SOME MUSINGS FROM THIS SIDE OF HEAVEN

Most of our missionary family who worked together closely over the years in India are now residing within easy reach of each other in Pennsylvania. We used to be quite a contingent but our number continues to decrease as one by one the Lord calls us home.

When Allen and I settled in Elizabethtown in mid-1981, Dr. Lowell Mann was one of the very first to grasp my hand as we entered church on our first Sunday. With his crooked but attractive smile, he said, "I know which Sunday school class wants you," and he led us directly into his! Yesterday morning, when we surprised many by our presence in the morning church service in Elizabethtown, both of our "Indian" doctors—Lowell Mann and Henry Kreider—came straight to us with big smiles on their faces, firm handshakes, and comments of joy at our being there once again.

The bonding remains. Even as the years pass, and our group decreases in number, those who are left find that the bonds strengthen regardless of time or circumstance. Most surely they will be strong in heaven, too.

When we left Elizabethtown last June to come to Messiah Village, one of the first to welcome us here was our dear sister in the Lord, Leora Yoder, also a former missionary to India. Leora preceded us to that land by less than two years. An exceptional missionary, she truly loved both her work and the people. As a missionary nurse who ran a clinic in Saharsa for many years, she

From left to right: Marietta Smith, Leoda and Allen Buckwalter, Erma Hare, and Leora Yoder.

quickly earned the name "the Doctor Missahib." The caring quality of her ministry throughout the almost four decades of her service in India is easily seen by two facts. Even in retirement she maintained contacts with former orphanage girls who needed relatives, someone who cared. Leora gave them that assurance. Also, while serving as Superintendent of Nurses in the mission hospital in Madhipura, she gave everybody a birth date, spreading the dates arbitrarily throughout the year. (Many people didn't know the month or day of their birth.) Then, each month she threw a special birthday party for those who had a "birthday." That was just like Leora!

We weren't surprised to have her welcome us to Messiah Village almost before anyone else. She has always had a special place in our hearts, and the fact that she was "Leora" and I am "Leoda" meant that many times our names were interchanged, both in India by missionary colleagues and here by those who knew us. It didn't bother us. It was simply a fact.

Life at Messiah Village can be either very full or very empty. Ours and hers were full. She volunteered her services throughout the years of her residence here. In fact, one reason she opted to move from an independent living situation to Assisted Living in October 1996 was to make mobility easier throughout the winter, so that she could come to "work" each day!

Our first four months were dedicated to finishing my manuscript, and to that end I made few exceptions for extra curricular activities. But Monday evenings were quickly set aside for Leora to come and play Scrabble, a game she loved. We soon learned that she enjoyed it so much, she was constantly looking for others with some degree of expertise.

Scrabble is the one game Allen and I have played together. He plays to win; I play for enjoyment. One evening when he came to bed late, I wondered what kept him so long. Next morning he told me he was counting up our total scores for the last fifty games we had played!

I was intrigued. "How did it turn out?" I quizzed.

Would you believe it? Fifty-fifty! Twenty four for him, the same for me, and two draws.

So Leora joined in the fun here, and much of the time Allen won, with Leora and I coming in second and third. One day she mentioned to me that she thought Allen had the advantage because he used the little electronic Scrabble dictionary in which he delighted as a time saver. I knew how she felt because I, too, had initially felt the same way until he assured me of his purpose—that he did not use it to find new words, but merely looked up the spelling of those words he thought up himself. Thus assured, I could tell her again of his integrity.

But the last Monday we played together, just less than 72 hours before the Lord called her to her heavenly home, Allen did not use his little device and time-saver. And Leora won! I can see her standing, thanking us for a most pleasant evening, and saying with that sweet, gentle smile that characterized her entire life and ministry, "Thank you for letting me win!"

That was Monday evening, January 26, 1998. On Thursday when she didn't appear for lunch, her neighbor went to investigate Leora's absence. She found our beloved sister sitting in her chair, lap robe in place, her soul in heaven, her body here!

One tribute after another poured in at the memorial service held on February 1, 1998. I didn't speak. I couldn't, for the suddenness of her homegoing shocked me through and through. Yet who could wish her back? She was with her beloved Lord, and even as she had preceded us to India in 1937, and was here to meet us at Messiah Village when we came in 1997, so now she has gone on before to glory to welcome us when our home-call comes.

How far are we from eternity, friend?

Let me assure you, just one heart-beat away! That's a sobering fact. But there's much to assure us that although yesterday has gone, and tomorrow may never come, now is ours to redeem. As I see it, the mandate is clear from the Lord of the Church. He says, "Behold, I come quickly." And elsewhere, we are told to "occupy" until he comes. Say with me, even as does John the Revelator in his concluding words, "Come quickly, Lord Jesus."